HABANOS

HABANOS

THE STORY OF THE HAVANA CIGAR

TEXT AND PHOTOGRAPHS BY
NANCY STOUT

RIZZOLI
NEW YORK

To Maria Elena Martín and Nuria Oquendo

I would like to warmly thank my friends, Cubaphiles Ron McGee, Jane Rubin, Mary Arda, Ned Sublette, and Ernesto Pujol for fanning spiritual fires; Dr. Alberto Bustamante, Luis Mejia, and Steve Ashley for their help in the early days of the project; my editor, David Morton; and all the people noted in the chapters.   N. S.

First published in the United States of America in 1997 by
Rizzoli International Publications, Inc.
300 Park Avenue South, New York NY 10010

Library of Congress Cataloging-in-Publication Data

Stout, Nancy
Habanos : the story of the Havana cigar / text and photographs by
Nancy Stout
p.   cm.
Includes bibliographical references
ISBN 0–8478–2006–8 (hc)
1. Cigars. 2. Cigar industry—Cuba—Havana—History.
TS2260. S78   1997
679' .72'097291—dc21   97–15445
                                CIP

Designed by Ingrid Castro

Printed and bound in Great Britain

Endpapers: Comandante Che Guevara knew the pleasure of a good cigar. Photographed in 1961 during the early years of the revolution. (Photograph by Raul Corrales)

Previous pages: This box of La Prueba cremas, manufactured by B. Menendez y Hno. at Habana Street No. 906, in Old Havana dates from the 1940s. (Collection: Tobacco Museum, Havana)

CONTENTS

PREFACE

Previous Pages: From the roof of the Santa Isabel Hotel on the Plaza des Armes in Old Havana, one looks from Segundo Cabo palace (left), to Real Fuerza fortress (center), and beyond to El Morro castle (back).

The Sarah Drugstore has been an institution in Old Havana for many years (*facing page*).

Throughout the world and throughout the history of the existence of cigars, there has been one, and one only, that has been recognized by the true connoisseur as the ultimate cigar, the legendary and peerless one, the *ne plus ultra*, and that is the *habano*. *Habanos* are cigars produced only in Cuba, shipped only from the port of Havana, made entirely of special varieties of Cuban-grown tobacco, and marketed only by the designated name *habano*.

They are smoked by the most famous people and sold for the highest prices. They are imitated and counterfeited. And, always, as the true sign of a rare luxury item, supply sometimes cannot meet demand, and they are often simply "N/A," not available.

Havana cigars have been N/A in the United States since the imposition of the blockade by President Kennedy in 1962. We get to smoke the imitated and counterfeited ones, or fine cigars from other countries. The irony is that Cubans do not smoke them either; *habanos* can only be purchased in Cuba in U.S. dollars, and most Cubans don't have extra dollars. On the other hand, Cubans are not cigarless; they are able to buy four national cigars per month at their local bodega, in pesos, on a ration card. These are called *tabacos*, which simply means "cigars" in Cuba, and they are made of rejected leaf. All other tobacco, that is, the very best, goes into cigars for export, the *habanos*.

Officially, *habanos* must meet five conditions. *Fundamental*: That the cigars be manufactured of tobacco, cultivated on a large scale, of particular varieties grown in Cuba. *Origen*: That the cigars are manufactured in Cuba. *Materia prima*: That the tobacco used is of high quality and the filler is necessarily of large leaves. *Proceso industrial*: That the product is made entirely by hand. *Garantia Oficial*: That the product is presented in foreign markets as guaranteed by the Cuban government, bearing a legal seal.

Knowledge of *habanos*, for a whole generation of Americans and Cubans, whether for political or financial reasons, is still a pretty nebulous thing. What, for instance, does a Cohiba cigar—a brand so sought after that it is rare and expensive even in Havana—taste like? You cannot rely entirely on the older generation who "knew" Havana cigars before the Revolution because some of the blends have changed. The heavy, sweet cigars of the 1950s are anathema to the dry, distilled power of the Cohiba developed in the 1960s. Now, every cigar smoker wants a box of Cohibas, but there are not enough produced to fill the demand. They are a luxury item in limited supply, and the same is true for the Montecristo and Romeo y Julieta blends. The European, Middle Eastern, and Asian cigar market pretty much dictates their availability and taste.

If *habanos*, with their mythical status and rarity, remain largely unknown, then cigar factories remain largely unseen. People in Havana do not know much about the famous factories and often confuse them with places for cigarette production, except for the La Corona factory, which is open to the public, and Partagás, which is not. These are hard to miss, though, since one is located at the base of the Presidential Palace, now the Museum of the Revolution, and the other is behind the Capitol Building, now the Academy of Sciences. But where were all the other factories? I had earlier roamed most of the streets and neighborhoods of Havana for months, photographing its architecture. Yet I felt that a certain mystery surrounded the cigar industry. I searched the streets convinced that there were unmarked cigar factories everywhere; I just had to find them.

The year I began to work on this book, 1994, exceptionally heavy rains fell during the growing season. Industry officials, preoccupied and fearful of the effects of the weather, encouraged me to delay my research until another season. Not wanting to wait, I argued that tobacco leaves were just one part of the story. I found an ally in Eusebio Leal, the Historian of the City, who understood my obsession with the streets and buildings of Havana and my desire to discover what lay behind these world-famous cigar factories. He admitted that he, too, had always felt a fascination for the industry but only knew it secondhand. He gave me a letter of endorsement and assigned a translator, Nuria Oquendo Arroyo, from his office to get me over the rough spots in the research libraries and at the factories. Thus equipped, and with the required licenses from the U.S. Treasury Department, I was given an opportunity rarely available to North Americans: I could snoop around Havana and its environs unimpeded.

I scoured the libraries for books about Havana cigars and was surprised to find only one, *Havana Cigars* by William Gill, similar to what I had in mind. It was written in 1910, so I thought an update would be timely.

In Cuba it is customary to enjoy a mid-morning cigar; the man here is smoking a lunchtime cigar at the Gringo Viejo restaurant in Vedado, Havana.

In Cuba, there have always been official tobacco historians: in this century, José Rivero Muñiz wrote three books between 1946 and 1964; José Perdomo compiled a wonderful lexicon in 1940; and Antonio Nuñez Jimenez currently produces books for Cubatabaco and Tabacalera, Madrid. In addition, two scholars have looked at the industry: Gaspar Garcia Gallo, in a two-volume work produced in 1961; and an Englishwoman, Jean Stubbs, whose 1985 doctoral dissertation examines the agro-industrial complex between 1860 and 1959. Everybody's favorite book, including my own, is *Cuban Counterpoint: Tobacco and Sugar* by Fernando Ortiz, published in 1936.

Most of these authors have an obsessive interest in defending Cuba's claim as the creator of "rolled leaves" and as the earliest recorded place where

The sight of women smoking, like these on Infanta Street in Central Havana, is not uncommon in Cuba.

tobacco was found. There are volumes of history analyzing fifteenth- and sixteenth-century references. On the other hand, there are style books on smoking by tobacco connoisseurs such as F.W. Fairholt, an Englishman writing in 1859 when cigars were still relatively new in London. In all the books two things are clear: one, cigars made of Cuban-grown tobacco are legendary because of their superior flavor and aroma; and two, there have always been imitations, which all the authorities admonish readers to avoid.

I learned to ignore imitators' labels, no matter how gilded. The twenty-dollar boxes of Cohibas in the streets of Havana are not genuine. Counterfeit *habanos* date back to the sixteenth century when Cuban tobacco was the exclusive privilege of Spanish kings; all other cigars were unauthorized and usually contraband. Pirates and buccaneers craved the lucrative *habano* and would do anything to obtain it in their raids along the Cuban coasts. In fact, until fairly recently, tobacco was part of an illicit trade outside the official relationship between Cuba and Spain. In the United States, the politics of trade agreements intrude on our smoking habits even today; in New York one could overhear in conversation, "I get tobacco from a reliable source smuggled directly from Havana." Such a statement could also have been made in Elizabethan England four hundred years ago.

For centuries the world hungered for well-crafted cigars, and around 1820, when the Spanish finally let the Cubans export *habanos* to countries other than Spain, Europeans and Americans were instant buyers. Those shipped directly from the port of Havana have always been guaranteed to be authentic. Better still are cigars boxed, sealed, and bearing a label with the exporter's name and address, which promises accountability.

Cubans themselves rarely claim they have the best tobacco in the world. Rather, they wisely let the rest of the world say it. Cuban literature on agriculture simply quotes the references, the U.S. Department of Agriculture among them, that come to this conclusion, and first-place medals garnered in competitions all over the world during the nineteenth and early twentieth centuries confirm it.

In the early days of the export cigar, women smoked as well as men. We know this because tobacco connoisseurs compiled albums of watercolors and engravings of snuff-taking and pipe-smoking men: suddenly, around 1830, these began to depict women with cigars. Women, also, have traditionally been key players in the cigar industry, though this has not always been recognized. Although black women were tobacco sellers in Columbus's day, and women played an important role when the cigar market billowed in the nineteenth century, and were leaf selectors in the growing areas, only men were in the rolling departments. In the 1960s, Celia Sanchez brought women in as rollers, and today they make up over half of the rollers in Havana. The Cohiba factory is the outcome of one of Sanchez's many projects to employ women. One of her missions was to find professions for the ninety thousand maids—and probably as many prostitutes—in Havana during the first decade of the revolution.

In my frequent and inquisitive trips around Havana, I have never been asked where I was going or what I was doing. This does not mean that the bureaucratic arm of the export cigar industry, the state-owned company Habanos, S.A., was not curious about what I was up to. I knew that I was breaking some rules. For instance, I visited some factories normally off limits to outsiders; but after conferences and phone calls to Habanos, S.A., I was always welcomed. Looking back, I feel that this had very little to do with security. It is more likely that visitors are seen as disruptive to the manufacturing process, especially now, when there is an all-out effort to increase production. As G. Cabrera Infante says in *Holy Smoke*, "To make a cigar is a devil of a skill, but to roll so many in a day's work is sheer sorcery." Even though the rolling rooms are the size of gymnasiums, they seem intimate and have a family atmosphere that is easily disturbed, especially since Cubans have an immense curiosity about outsiders.

As it happened, I was visiting the Romeo y Julieta factory just days after the Cubans had shot down two small planes that had flown into their air space from the United States. Our two countries were firing hostile accusations toward each other hourly. I held my breath as I was introduced over the microphone as a North American writer. The rollers broke into applause. For an instant I felt my throat tighten and thought tears would come into my eyes. Later, I decided they were delighted that I'd come with a letter from Eusebio

Leal. People love his weekly television program, on which he walks through the city and talks about its history; they want to be, like him, aficionados of Havana's history. Leal also secures resources from institutions throughout the world for restoration of Old Havana, and, perhaps because of this, is a friend of Fidel.

I have met Fidel. At a reception, I shook a hand softer and better manicured than my own, and with slightly longer nails. I am tall, but I had to look up. Fidel is perhaps six feet seven inches in his military boots, and was by far the tallest person in the room. I was introduced to him in 1992, while working on my book on Havana architecture. Cubans noticed in that book that I often ignore the usual landmarks. Consequently, Habanos, S.A. didn't expect me to stick to their view of the cigar industry and didn't try to make me follow it. I frequently stopped by their offices to ask questions. I knew they were keeping an eye on my progress and assumed they were monitoring my routes as I worked the city with my lists and map.

Each day I methodically traveled to addresses I had taken from a 1940s list of cigar manufacturers. I also had a short list of factories from the 1978 telephone directory, the most recent one until a new edition was published in 1996. I annotated my map with ink spots, except when I found holes in blocks where a building once stood. Some days I came across ghosts of the past—buildings standing empty as though waiting for something to change. Other times I discovered factories that are now tobacco warehouses. Good days revealed vital, efficient factories that have never changed. I also located a group of buildings, not on any list, that are tobacco warehouses.

In most of the literature on smoking, cigar smokers go to private clubs, drink, and smoke one good cigar. This may be how they used to do it, but in reality private clubs were banned with the revolution, food on occasion is scarce, wine is a luxury, and if only one cigar is available, Cubans smoke it after breakfast, not dinner! In the morning rush hour, commuters on bicycles and policemen on motorcycles smoke cigars. In my months in Havana, I learned all the nuances of cigar smoking behavior.

A smoker takes a break in the opulent Casa de Amistad on Paseo Street in Vedado, Havana.

One hot morning, en route to the farmers market, I walked down Paseo, an avenue that has very large trees in the center and old iron and wood-slatted benches left over from the Republican period. I stopped to rest and shared a bench with a man smoking a cigar. He was reading a novel and didn't look up. His cigar was bigger than a government-issued breva, but not an expensive export model either. It seemed to be of little concern to him. Much of the time it rested in his hand, which was on his knee; then it was brought to his mouth, puffed gently several times and returned to rest. At one point the cigar stayed in the reader's mouth and both hands held the novel, *Gallego* by Miguel Barnet.

A man came up and interrupted the reader to ask for a light for his cigarette. The reader didn't offer his cigar, but reached into his pocket for a lighter and quickly returned to reading. After the man went away, the reader removed the ashes from his cigar. Had the man had a cigar and not a cigarette,

the reader very well might have raised his eyes, searched the man's face, put the novel down, if only briefly, knocked the ashes from his cigar and offered it for a light. He might even have spoken a word or two, but that he did not illustrates that cigar smokers are seen as superior in Cuba. Based on the smoking hierarchy, it is understood that the one would ignore the other; this is, after all, still the country where the first cigarettes were made from sweepings from cigar factory floors and referred to as "dirty."

I had been so dazzled by wrapper leaves, after seeing the tall plants grown under the shade of acres of gauzy white cloth in the Vuelta Abajo, that I couldn't conceptualize the rest of the cigar. Then Esther Luisa Hernandez, one of Cuba's great rollers, explained that each cigar is both recipe and ingredients, outer brocade and inner lining, and that the roller is both chef and tailor. The cigar is an object and a symbol. Therefore, I begin this book with Esther. In the first chapter, "The Art of the Cigar," she explains the slow and very careful process of making each cigar, which I hope will fill your mind with the aroma, the taste, and the feel of tobacco leaves, and evoke a sense of the cigar's extraordinary five-hundred-year history.

A word of caution, though. After five hundred years, the Cuban cigar industry has packaged its story very smoothly. I have tried to give you an appendix to that story. If I had not read historian Jean Stubbs, I would not have known how precarious the industry had become at the turn of the century. If I had not read ethnographer Fernando Ortiz, I would not know about the intrigues among sailors and women, Indians and blacks, to popularize tobacco. If I had not seen an illustration of a lynching—tobacco farmers hanging from trees—in a book of poetry and later in a child's history book, the legacy of the tobacco monopoly would not have sunk in.

Discovering the *Cartilla Rústica*, which I found in the Rare Book Room of the New York Public Library after searching every library in Havana, gave me the most pleasure. If there is a bible of tobacco growing, this is it. Written in 1840 as a dialogue between a father and son, it contains all of the myths and practices of tobacco in one little treatise. It is a primer of growing practices and a key to much of the symbolism on cigar box labels. My visit with Alejandro Robaina, Cuba's preeminent grower, only confirms that very little has changed in the way that Cuban tobacco has been grown and cured since the *Cartilla Rústica* was written. This is perhaps the main reason why Havana cigars have maintained their legendary place throughout history.

One of the perks of cigar rolling is the use of company tobacco to customize one's own cigars, like this roller, smoking her personally crafted cigar at the H. Upmann factory in Old Havana.

Selecting cigars for color is an exacting task, as seen here at Partagás.

All factories have a "cabinet," or storage and aging room; this one is at Partagás.

Overleaf: The rolling rooms, a central part of the factories, are naturally well-ventilated but keep light levels low. This one at the former Romeo y Julieta factory, now called Antonio Briones Montoto, in Central Havana is an exception.

THE ART OF THE CIGAR

Esther Luisa Hernandez is one of Cuba's great tobacco rollers. She is a tall, slender, African-Cuban woman. Her hands are delicate, with glossy skin like polished wood, and her nails are painted light pink, the color of summer roses. She wears large glasses that sit in the middle of the bridge of her nose. She was in the process of making a julieta, a fairly large cigar, when I met her at the Romeo y Julieta factory.

The room she works in has fluorescent light overhead and natural light from a long wall lined with opened windows. A soft breeze sweeps across the rolling tables. Unlike most cigar factories, which are dim places where dark green window blinds are drawn so the tobacco stays damp, in this one the cinnamon leaves mix with a fresh breeze. I fuss with my camera and try to put the three feet of my tripod in a place where they don't fit. Finally, I simply stand in front of Esther, my elbows leaning on her table, and watch. She smiles at this decision.

As she worked she told me that she had been rolling cigars for twenty-five years and had been awarded a commemorative cigar in recognition of her work. "My mother rolled cigars in a factory, in Pinar del Rio." She told me that her mother had been recognized for her skill as a roller as well.

"Let me show you how I roll cigars." It is a simple invitation.

"There are three varieties of leaves that make up the filler, the *tripa*, of a cigar." I'd seen this done a hundred times before. Was it the sunlight that made the leaves on her table look so different? The rolling appeared to be in slow motion.

"I take two leaves of *el seco tripa*, dry filler, for flavor. I add half a leaf of *ligero*, light, to give the cigar strength," and she tore one leaf in half and pressed it into her palm along with the two dry filler leaves. I understand that she is teaching me a recipe—she is telling me how cigars are blended.

"You also need one leaf of *volado* for combustion."

She wraps a binder around the julieta, trims it, and puts it into a mold. Now she turns her attention again to me. "You wanted to know about the cigars I smoke?" I tell her that I'd been learning about smoking habits in Havana by asking a lot of questions.

"My own cigars are softer; the ones I make for myself." She pauses. "I'll make one for you." We start again. She chooses two leaves from the Romeo y Julieta blend on her table. They are thick, but soft and spongy. She takes the other half-leaf left over from the julieta, then picks up two dark and thick *volado* leaves. I watch the *volado* go into the center of the leaves already cupped in her hand.

"Those are two *volado*," I protest, and ask for clarification, thinking, "How can she use two leaves of fire?"

Then she put the long filler leaves down on her table lengthwise, folding and compressing them together in a roll. "This does not change the flavor. I've reduced the *ligero* proportionately by adding more fire. A roller may add more of any of the three ingredients. It depends on the leaves before her." I like the way she speaks as though all rollers are women.

I smoked one of her cigars later that day. It burned comfortably fast, easily and well, and it certainly was *not* a bland cigar, despite her "soft" description. Although bigger than a panatela, and a little smaller than a breva, I smoked it in about twenty minutes.

She returns to making julietas. I concentrate on the *capote*, the binder. This is one of the two outer leaves on the cigar, similar in texture to the outer wrapper.

"This leaf is like an inner lining in a dress." She takes a knife and trims the well-shaped body to size. The filler leaves left over from the cut are brushed aside.

Esther takes the *capote*-wrapped cigar—called a "bunch"—and puts it into a mold, a *tabla*. Every table has a stack of molds shaped for the type of cigar being rolled. A young man comes by to pick up the molds and carries them to a press.

"Is every cigar put in a mold?"

"Depending on the *vitola* [the size and shape of the cigar]. All large cigars are put in a mold. They remain there for a period of time, not particularly long—in some cases only ten minutes. They settle and shape." We look at the molds stacked up in a press. The young man tightens the press by hand.

"The press is not about shape, it is about good density. The press makes internal combustion of the tobacco good."

Esther Luisa Hernandez, one of Cuba's greatest tobacco rollers, practices her craft at Romeo y Julieta.

Other women join us for a few moments from time to time. We are mother and daughter, teacher and student. There is a hum in the factory, but not from machines. People converse quietly, from table to table and along the aisles, with their supervisors and friends.

Esther opens a package of *capa*, or wrapper leaves. In the Romeo y Julieta factory these are distinctly brown, flecked with gold. In Havana, unfolding squares of plastic containing *capa* leaves is rather like seeing gems uncovered at a jeweler. It seems impossible not to stare for a moment. She gently smoothes a *capa* leaf, spreading it out on her table, then trims along the outer edge of the leaf.

I think about what I'd learned in Pinar del Rio. Nearly all the energies of growing shade tobacco—developing these big, pale green leaves, grown under miles of cheesecloth, tied up with thousands of yards of string so the plants stand perfectly straight, like ballerinas—go into these wrapper leaves. Good wrappers are like silk, extremely soft, with fine veins more like delicate webs than a vegetable structural system. Esther's wrapper felt like oiled tissue paper.

"The *capa* is the cigar's outside dress." I know that the capa is a leaf that is selected for visual appeal, an expensive outer layer. She takes the body of the cigar from the pressed mold and lays it down on the *capa*.

"Begin at the end of the cigar that is lighted and finish at the end that goes in the mouth." She rolls the *capa* in a spiral around the body. Then with her knife she cuts out a little circle of tobacco, about the size of a nickel. She touches a tiny dot of vegetable paste to the circle, and then, placing it over the head of the cigar with her thumbs, she smoothes the completely enclosed head, the *casquillo*. She holds the cigar for a moment, then compares it to a gauge on the table to check its length. With a *chaveta*, a knife without a handle and with a short, moon-shaped blade, she trims the end to the proper length, pushing aside the spare tobacco.

The cigar is finished. It is unique. She, however, is proud that it looks like all the others. As if she knows what I'm thinking, the great roller sums up her work: "Of course, the *art* of the cigar is always about individual perfection achieving uniformity."

In the quality control department the cigars will be sorted by color and shape, and men and women will select the twenty-five nearly identical cigars that go into a box. Each row will be carefully arranged so that no two cigars will contrast sharply. The ringer will lift each cigar out of the box, never changing the order, never rotating the cigar, and will paste the paper ring around the head of the cigar and return it to the box, exactly as found. All this is done in the name of individual perfection achieving uniformity.

Esther Luisa Hernandez trims the edge of the *capa*, the outer wrapper leaf of the cigar (*top*). Then she dresses the cigar with the *capa* after it comes from a pressed mold (*center*). Finally, she encloses the head of the cigar, the *casquillo*, before trimming it with a *chaveta*, a moon-shaped blade (*bottom*).

Overleaf: Some of the world's finest tobacco is produced in the fields outside San Juan y Martínez in the Vuelta Abajo, Pinar del Rio Province.

ESTRECHO DE L
Straits of Flor

GOLFO DE MEXICO
Gulf of Mexico

CAYOS
BANCO SALADO
Salt Key Bank

Nicholas Chann

BAHIA HONDA

MARIEL

HABANA

MATANZAS

CÁRDENAS

PINAR DEL RIO

HABANA

CARRETERA CENTRAL

MATANZAS

P. DE ZAPATA

SANTA CLARA

CIENFUEGOS

TRINIDAD

CANAL DE YUCATAN
Yucatan Channel

S. ANTONIO

GOLFO DE BATABANÓ
Gulf of Batabanó

ISLA DE PINOS
Isle of Pines

ESTACION EXPERIMENTAL DEL TABACO
TOBACCO EXPERIMENTAL STATION

MAR CA
Caribbean Sea

ZONAS O DISTRITOS TABACALEROS

VUELTA ABAJO y SEMI VUELTA (PROVINCIA DE PINAR DEL RIO)		PARTIDO (PROVINCIA DE LA HABANA Y PINAR DEL RIO)		REMEDIOS PROVINCIA DE SANTA CLARA Y CAMAGUEY		ORIENTE PROVINCIA DE ORIENTE
1	San Juan y San Luis	1	Tumbadero	1-A	Cabaiguan	1 Yara y Guisa.
2	El Llano	2	Caimito y Cayo La Rosa	1-B	Lomas	2 Mayari
3	Lomas	3	Govea Paletas y Piedras	1-C	Manicaragua	
4	Remates	4	Buenaventura	2	Placetas	
5	Guane	5	Artemisa	3	Santa Clara	
6	Mantua		(P. del R.)	4	Encrucijada Camajuani y Vueltas	
7	Costa Sur			5	Yaguajay	
8	Costa Norte			6	Esperanza Jicotea y Ranchuelo	
9	Semi-Vuelta			7	Tamarindo (P de C.)	

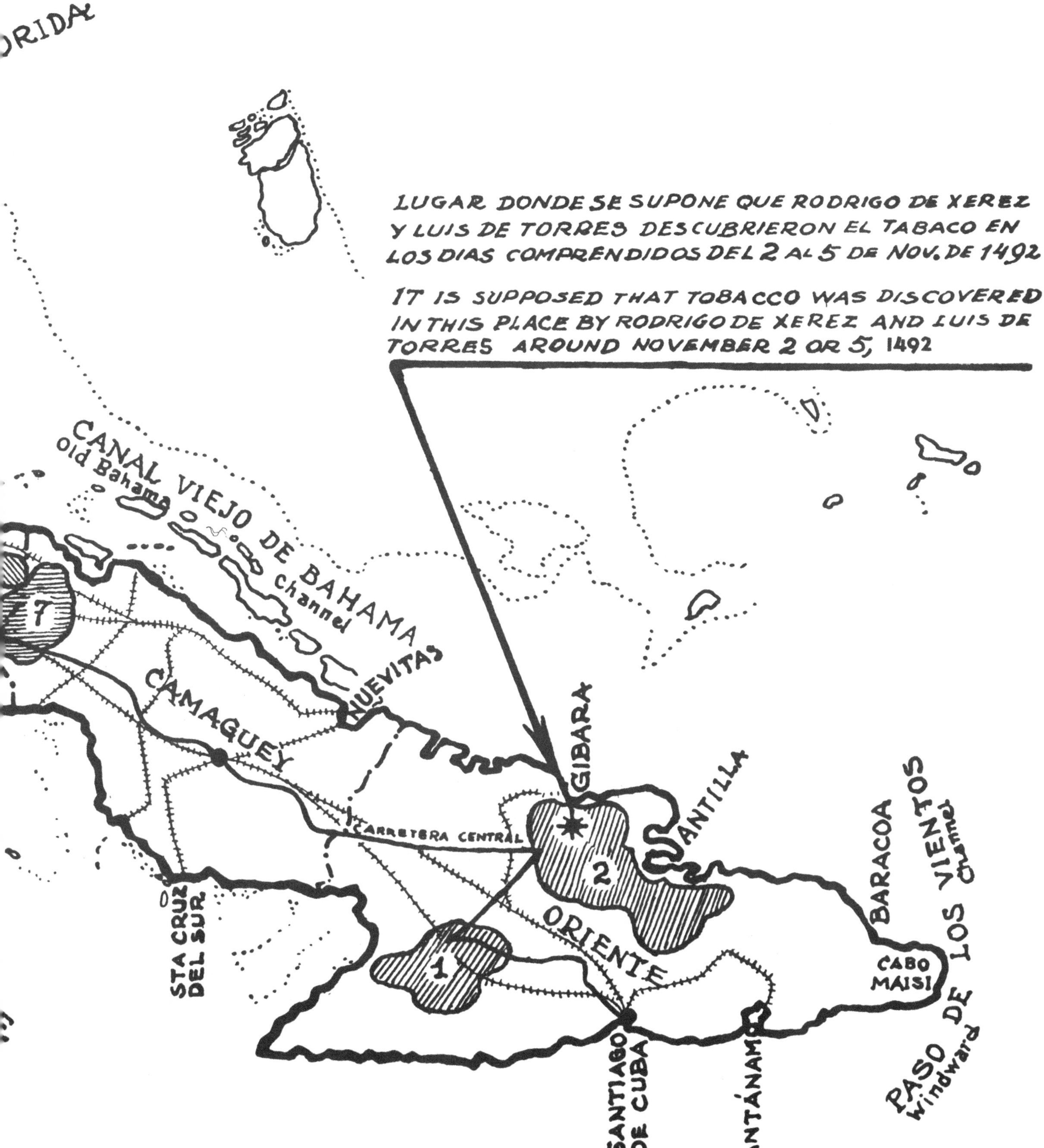

FLORIDA

LUGAR DONDE SE SUPONE QUE RODRIGO DE XEREZ Y LUIS DE TORRES DESCUBRIERON EL TABACO EN LOS DIAS COMPRENDIDOS DEL 2 AL 5 DE NOV. DE 1492

IT IS SUPPOSED THAT TOBACCO WAS DISCOVERED IN THIS PLACE BY RODRIGO DE XEREZ AND LUIS DE TORRES AROUND NOVEMBER 2 OR 5, 1492

CANAL VIEJO DE BAHAMA
Old Bahama Channel

NUEVITAS

CAMAGUEY

STA CRUZ DEL SUR

CARRETERA CENTRAL

GIBARA

ANTILLA

ORIENTE

BARACOA

CABO MAISI

PASO DE LOS VIENTOS
Windward Channel

SANTIAGO DE CUBA

GUANTÁNAMO

HABANOS

VERGARA

25 - ELEGANTES - 25
EN
CAJITAS DE 5 HABANOS

THE VEGAS

THE VUELTA ABAJO
AND ALEJANDRO ROBAINA

From the earliest period of settlement, Cuba has been divided into tobacco growing zones: the Vuelta Abajo, the Semivuelta, the Partido, and the Vuelta Arriba. These zones extend from Pinar del Rio in the west to Santiago on the eastern side of Cuba. The area known throughout the world for the finest tobacco is Vuelta Abajo, in the Pinar del Rio province directly west of Havana. The main street of the town of Pinar del Rio runs from the Havana highway past the Pinar del Rio Hotel and the Museum of Sciences, into the town's center, and continues uphill past such colorful but mundane establishments as the Red Paris barber shop, to meet Antonio Maceo Street at a triangular plaza. Just off the plaza is a cigar factory called the Vueltabajo. It is not a particularly distinguished factory, but since it is located in the heart of the most famous region of tobacco growers, buses arrive every day bringing tourists from all over the world. The building was originally a prison, and has the presence of a public building, its colonnaded facade matching the courthouse down the street. Visitors can enter the leaf selection room, the rolling gallery, a room with cedar cabinets where they select and age cigars, a tiny canteen in the courtyard, and two shops where cigars and souvenirs are sold.

My first trip was to San Juan y Martínez. From September through March, the highway from Pinar del Rio south is lined with fields of tobacco plants. As we approached the town, I was astonished by the sight of miles of fields under a fabric cover and rows of large barns that appeared to float on this sea of gently waving fabric. Just before entering San Juan y Martínez the road runs through a river valley where royal palm trees, trunks painted white, edge the highway. This is Hoya de Monterrey, the plantation founded by José Gener in the nineteenth century. The front gate is the only evidence of the plantation's former elegance. Inside is a small complex of high-rise apartment buildings to house the workers. Rubbish is everywhere. I felt a great sense of loss. For what? I am not entirely sure. The romance of the name, I guess. Later, when I found the beautiful old José Gener factory in Havana, unused by the tobacco industry, I experienced the same sense of disappointment.

Then, early one morning, I went to visit the tobacco farm of Alejandro Robaina at San Luis. To enter Robaina's farm we had to drive up a steep driveway, deeply rutted from the rains. The fields have very good drainage, since they are situated on a gradual slope, and the soil is a composition of gravel, sand, and clay. Robaina's operation is enormous: there are five large barns to be filled to capacity during the next two months. The farm has been owned by the Robaina family since 1846.

Robaina is eighty-three years old and has been in charge of the farm for forty-seven years. After touring one of the fields, Robaina invited me to his house to meet his wife, Teresa, and they showed me various clippings, mementos of journalists' visits to the farm, and a copy of *Cigar* magazine with Robaina's face on the cover. Inside, the article called him Cuba's leading tobacco grower.

"I come from a long line of tobacco growers. My grandfather was an excellent grower and my father, Maruto Robaina, was the best in the country." He handed me a snapshot. It was a picture of Robaina and the president of the country, flanked by government ministers, shaking hands at an awards ceremony in Havana. These souvenirs are well-thumbed and it gave the old man pleasure to show them to me. The real news, Robaina told me quietly but proudly, was that Fidel had been to the farm to discuss this year's crop only a few days before. The length of his visit was impressive, a confirmation of Robaina's status among farmers of the region. "Fidel spent over *thirty minutes* here," Robaina told each of us in turn.

On the morning I visited the farm, three people were working directly with tobacco plants. They wore plastic sheets wrapped around their waists, tied with rope, to help them move through the sticky, dew-drenched crop. One of the men who bent down to pick the lower leaves wore a plastic shower cap. A woman worker adjusting the strings on the plants wore a flower in her hair à la Billie Holiday. Altogether, Robaina has twenty employees, mostly workers who started their careers at the government experimental agricultural station a few miles away. Robaina is highly revered and is sent the best graduates—or so I was told. The other employees I saw that morning

Alejandro Robaina, Cuba's leading tobacco producer, holding a *capa* (outer wrapping leaf) at his farm in San Luis.

were a woman stringing up leaves in the barn, two men moving irrigation hoses, and another repairing a tractor. Not many people, but, as Cubans like to say, everything seemed under control.

Robaina believes his technique for growing shade tobacco is foolproof. He lavishes care on each plant: careful suckering—the removal of excess shoots along the stem of the plant—and a lavish use of string, wrapped and rewrapped around each stalk and pulled upward. His plants were already taller than all the people present, about six feet, and required thirty more days to mature and reach their full height of at least seven feet. He staggers the planting, transplanting the seedlings in groups to be able to attend to the plants individually. When I visited the farm he already had some of the mature leaves drying in the barns.

Robaina's older son will inherit the farm. His hair, like his father's, is crew-cut, but is still black. The effect is handsome, a little tough. He looks like a vigorous man in his forties, but the appearance was dispelled when he raised his shirt to show me a waist-to-neck scar from heart surgery. Teresa and Robaina's two white-haired sisters manage the house and a large flower garden. When I left, Teresa gave me two big orchids from this garden, and Robaina gave me a cigar, about eight inches long, rolled from his own personal selection of tobacco.

The main plant for receiving and grading the tobacco from the farms around the area is only a few miles away from Robaina's farm. Robaina's tobacco will be delivered there during the upcoming months before being shipped exclusively to the Cohiba factory in Havana. All the farms in the area grow shade tobacco under walls and ceilings of netting. Where one farm ends the next begins, the boundaries marked by narrow footpaths. Leaves are carried from the fields in large, shallow wicker baskets and loaded into trucks parked along the highway. The farms are old and famous. The most famous variety of Cuban wrapper tobacco, Corojo, was developed at El Corojo a few miles outside San Luis. Nothing is ostentatious. If you are lucky you might see a name on a gatepost.

When we arrived at the plant we were greeted by two women who gossiped about Fidel's visit. They asked me for a donation of three dollars and assigned a man to explain the major activities of the plant. Just inside the door, bundles of leaves were heaped in a long pile and were being sprinkled with water, put in a square cart, covered with burlap, and left to become moist throughout.

Tobacco from these carts is then taken into the huge sorting room. This is women's territory. Women of all ages perform the highly skilled work of sorting leaves and have done so for centuries. It is clearly a job that takes a good eye and a gentle touch. The sorting room resembled a schoolroom complete with rows of small tables and chairs all facing the front of the room, patriotic portraits, and a flag. Women sat at desks and unfolded the moist leaves carefully, one leaf at a time. Other women separated the wrapper leaves from the filler leaves and removed the stem and lower part of the vein. The graders

Previous pages: Workers must adjust the string supporting each plant in shade tobacco fields, as in this one owned by Alejandro Robaina (*left*).

To protect their clothing, field workers often wrap themselves in plastic, as this one at the farm of Alejandro Robaina, who is seen in the background (*right*).

At Alejandro Robaina's house, freshly picked shade tobacco leaves rest on a wrought iron table.

Unlike sun tobacco, freshly cut shade tobacco
leaves are strung on a pole and hung to dry in
a barn.

made stacks of similarly sized leaves, weighing the stacks down with boards. I have been told that much depends on sorting tobacco leaves for texture and color, yet looking back, there is never very much light in these rooms—only a greenish fluorescent light.

The stemmed and sorted leaves are collected and taken upstairs to the drying room, and all the scraps lying on the floor are collected. Every bit of tobacco is stripped from the veins and put into barrels to be shipped off to flavor cigarettes. The clean, branchlike veins will be used as mulch. Not one centimeter of this high-grade tobacco is wasted.

The second-floor drying room was filled with sunlight reflected off the white cloth covering the tobacco fields outside the building. The light in the room was bright but altered: nicotine had created a yellow film covering the windowpanes. This amber-colored light illuminated racks and racks of damp

Cured leaves are piled up at the Cooperativa Eusebio Gonzalez Llanos, a grading facility in San Luis where leaves are sorted by size, texture, and color.

Overleaf: A worker on the farm outside the Cooperativa Eusebio Gonzalez Llanos brings a basket of leaves from the field.

After the tobacco is graded, packed in palm bark (the only material that will not harm the tobacco), and covered in burlap, the entire bale of leaves is pressed and shipped to Havana.

tobacco leaves actively drying and fermenting in the heat. After a few moments I began to gasp—the nicotine was so strong. I was told that nobody can stay here more than a few minutes, but I insisted on doing so since I had brought my camera to photograph the nicotine-stained wooden racks, which have turned a beautiful shade of soft red, and which held trays from floor to ceiling. Everybody around me fled downstairs. I worked quickly, anxiety-filled and buzzed, and apparently disturbed the tripod since the picture is blurred.

When the leaves are considered to be dry enough, they are taken downstairs to the warehouse, where the leaves are parceled into hands of tobacco, then stacked in pyramids called *burros* and kept damp and hot while they

ferment for several months. Finally the *burros* are opened and the tobacco is packed into bales—called *tercios*—of about eighty bundles each. The bales are wrapped in water-soaked bark from the royal palm tree, which is pliable when wet and forms a sturdy packing case when it dries.

One of the bales, covered in burlap, was under a big press in the shipping room. There were strips of palm bark lying about. When I asked about it, one of the men knocked on the side of the bale to show that the palm bark had been used, explaining that it is the only material that is strong but flexible, and will not harm the tobacco. The burlap edges were sewn with a large needle and string, and a label was stuck on top of the bale, addressed to Havana.

Tobacco is kept in the entrance room of the Cooperativa Eusebio Gonzalez Llanos grading station before it is sorted.

Following pages: Following a tradition seen in many Hispanic cultures, the exteriors of houses, such these on Antonio Maceo Street in Pinar del Rio, are faced in beautiful patterned tile.

VIÑALES: THE HISTORIC CENTER

William Gill's *Havana Cigars* opens with an image of a cigar label. It pictures early morning on a *vega*, a tobacco field. The sun is rising over a mountain, a stream runs from the mountain through the fields in the center of the picture. *Vegueros*, tobacco farmers, cultivate the tobacco fields with oxen or by hand with a hoe. They wear white trousers and shirts, and narrow-brimmed straw hats with black ribbons. Their houses, not their barns, are shown in the picture, conveying a domestic grace. These modest houses, called *bohios*, were first used by Taino Indians and are roofed with the palm thatch indigenous to Cuba. Palm trees dot the landscape. Two tobacco plants in flower, their stems tied together with striped ribbon, frame the picture—the flowers will produce seeds, assuring future tobacco plants. Two cigar boxes and four cigar bundles lie in the foreground to remind you, the smoker, that the cigar in your hand came from this scene.

The Viñales valley looks like this cigar label. It is picturesque, with palm-thatched tobacco barns and houses often made of palm logs. The town of Viñales is charming. Its single street is lined with palm trees and is one of the main tourist attractions in Cuba. I walked the length of the town taking pictures. It was Sunday and I found many men smoking cigars and happy to pose. Women at a maternity hospital, waiting for Sunday visitors, called out to me. They all wanted to have their picture taken.

I wondered why the farmers in this valley weren't using cheesecloth to produce high-priced shade tobacco as they were thirty miles away in San Luis. Were they simply nostalgic? Throughout my travels in Pinar del Rio, shade tobacco was always described as superior and the word "inferior" was used to describe the little *vegas* where tobacco grew in front of the farmers' small houses.

Back in Havana I related my impressions to photographer Raul Corrales. He smiled, and the lesson began.

"Years ago, growers in the Viñales valley realized that the best leaf—large and pale—grew in the shade of the mountains." In Viñales I'd seen amazing mountains which seemed to rise from flat ground into sheer cliffs.

"The original famous *hoyas* [flatlands] were these pockets of shade in the valley which produced the truly great leaves. The mountains gave shadow to the plant throughout its life. Creating shade by using cheesecloth was an experimental outcome of this discovery.

"As you can imagine," he continued, "the most serious producers in San Juan y Martínez and San Luis wanted to employ this method for their cash

Previous Pages: The *hoyas* (flatlands) in the Viñales valley of the Semi Vuelta produce what is considered the sun tobacco, which is grown in the shade of the surrounding mountains.

The graphic quality of cigar labels has often been admired. This one decorates the frontispiece of *Havana Cigars* by William Gill, published in 1910.

Traditional methods are still used for preparing the soil of a sun-grown tobacco field in the Viñales Valley (*facing page*).

Mothers-to-be wait for their Sunday visitors at the maternity hospital on Viñales's only street

crop. By using the cheesecloth cover, the plants were protected from insects as well. It was finally possible to produce absolutely perfect wrapper leaves."

I remembered that experimental use of cheesecloth was introduced to the Vuelta Abajo by Luis Marx just before the turn of the century.

"Why hadn't everyone switched to shade tobacco?" I asked.

"Obviously, if this were the answer to raising good tobacco everyone would do it. Fine cigars are the result of a blend of different flavors. Shade tobacco alone does not make a good cigar."

We returned to geography. "You must go to other parts of the country and look at the different types of tobacco farms," he told me. "Travel to Las Villas and look at sun tobacco, *tabaco del sol*."

More fields and barns? The idea set my teeth on edge.

"The sun is what burns up the leaves, makes them stronger in flavor," he insisted.

I said I really didn't think I had time, since I had so much to do in Havana to locate all the places that are significant to cigar manufacturing—I'd barely started. Just getting around the city is a nightmare. I couldn't afford to take tourist taxis, and the public buses are jammed during the morning rush hour. Every day was spent flagging down cars, figuring out routes, and making deals for rides. I'd seen the most famous shade tobacco farms already and had no time to waste touring the seemingly less significant sun tobacco farms.

Corrales was unimpressed by my tirade. "Shade makes the leaves bigger and milder, perfect for cigar wrappers. But sun gives the cigar flavor, makes it burn." Corrales poured a glass of rum, waiting for my storm of resistance to pass over.

I mellowed out and picked up my notebook. Cuban cigars do taste wonderful. I thought of the beautiful, expensive cigars I'd bought in New York, with reputable names, that sometimes tasted just like cardboard.

"The flavor of a cigar is determined by the location of the farm where the tobacco was grown. From location you will learn about the flavors of the blends."

In Havana I had been interviewing cigar smokers, asking what brand of cigar they had smoked before the Revolution. Many people recalled Cazadores, which were produced by Bauza in Manicaragua. Cazadores and H. Upmann No. 4s had been Corrales' favorite cigars, and he had smoked twelve daily. "I always liked a sweet cigar dressed in tobacco from Las Villas." I got out my map and underlined Manicaragua, located in the middle of the island. He also urged me to travel northward to Remedios, enticing me by saying that "the old smokers of the best cigars occasionally—very, very occasionally—tasted a hint of salt in the tobacco that grew near the sea."

I asked him to tell me more. On the map he pointed to an area in the Pinar del Rio province along the coast. Tobacco grown there must be influenced by the sea air. Later, at the Cohiba factory, I asked for a list of the locations where they procure their tobacco. After raising their eyebrows at the nerve of such a question, they gave me the list. Dimas, on the coast, was one of the locations.

Corrales continued, "The old brands had all these flavors. You purchased the ones you liked to smoke, depending on the blend. The black tobacco of Bayamo and Santiago, for example, is strong, and some people prefer brands made with it." He insisted that by visiting Camajuani, Cabaiguan, and Manicaragua—all towns near Santa Clara in the Las Villas province—I would learn to respect the old blends, even though many of these blends no longer exist.

"Remember, Nancy: Havana cigars are really about geography."

This building at the edge of Viñales's square is typical of the town's charm, which makes it one of the main tourist attractions in Cuba.

Overleaf: In the famous growing area called the Vuelta Abajo, tobacco farms line the road between San Juan y Martínez and San Luis.

The Vuelta Arriba:
Growing *Tabaco Del Sol* in Manicaragua, Camajuani, Remedios, and Cabaiguan

I had been watching the national baseball playoff games on television. The best teams were Villa Clara from the Las Villas province and the Industriales from Havana. My favorite player, Osmany Garcia, was from Villa Clara. The stadiums provided live music throughout the games, and when the games were held in Santa Clara cow bells and *claves* always sustained a high energy level. I decided to stop there on my way to the great sun tobacco farms of the Vuelta Arriba.

The road from Havana to Santa Clara, built by the Russians, runs in a straight line, and does not, it so happens, intersect with even one town on the 153-mile route. Sugarcane grows at the edge of this six-lane highway for most of those miles. Setting the fields on fire is one technique for harvesting cane. It burns off the leaves and makes cutting with the huge mechanical harvesters easier. I traveled through intermittent infernos that day—the air black with smoke, workers at the road's edge covered in soot from the burning leaves—only to emerge on the other side where the air was pristine. At the end of this surreal journey I encountered Santa Clara, an old and prosperous city.

The center of Santa Clara is said to have a greater number of colonial buildings—dating from 1689, when Santa Clara was founded, through 1850—per square mile than Havana. The town's social history was explained to me by the city librarian, Judith Quesada, who was proud of the city and its colonial architecture, but satisfied with the spirit of the Revolution as well.

"At the core of all Spanish towns is a Parque Central, where people meet to discuss important issues. The old Parque Central in Santa Clara was noted for its beauty and its unusual landscape design, which consisted of two concentric pathways. White people walked on the inner path, and black people on the outside with the firm understanding that they should never diagonally cross to the inner circle. The Revolution of 1959 came and went. The decree of racial equality was taught, but nothing happened about the two paths. Citizens of Santa Clara were instructed to make cultural changes, but black people did not feel confident enough of the new revolution to step into the inner path, or indeed walk from the Santa Clara Libre Hotel across the

Santa Clara lies in the heart of the Vuelta Arriba, where the great sun tobacco farms are located. The town dates from 1689 and is known for its colonial buildings. The neoclassical building on the main square is now the public library (*facing page*).

The opulence of the library's interior contrasts the serene classicism of the building's facade (*above*).

park to the public library. Therefore, in the 1960s, the town planners decided to relandscape the park, creating one large pavement, even though they had to sacrifice some of the ancient trees and the beauty of the older plantings."

Now the park is a major rendezvous, especially at night, among all sorts and ages of people. It was pleasant to sit with a drink in the rooftop bar of the pockmarked Santa Clara Libre Hotel (there are still bullet holes from the days when Radio Rebelde, rebel radio, broadcast from its roof).

About five blocks away, where Independence Street crosses the Cubanicay River, local farmers, construction workers, and farm-machinery dealers made a monument from the train that Commandante Che Guevara derailed. It was Che's main military exercise, and it successfully stopped Batista's troops on December 28, 1958. The city librarian gave me a map that had a picture of Che on its cover and the city coat of arms on the back: a castle, a key, and a tobacco barn and field are surrounded by the words "country," "prosperity," and "family."

South of Santa Clara is the pretty old tobacco town of Manicaragua. A tobacco factory for hand-rolling national cigars called Selectos is located in the center of town. A bronze plaque honoring Che Guevara and his rebel army (*ejercito rebelde*) of the Escambray Mountains, which are visible in the distance, is mounted on a marble column nearby.

Alberto Peres Hernandez from the Empressa Acopio y Benificio de Tabacos Manicaragua agreed to show me his export tobacco. We went to a large whitewashed building containing the best of the sun tobacco, *tabaco del sol*. Two women were grading leaves. A bright light was suspended directly above the opened *burro* of steamy tobacco bundles. The women fanned out each little bouquet of leaves, checking for mildew, eliminating bundles in which the color of the leaves varied too greatly, or the leaves were spotted. Anything less than perfect was placed in a pile for national consumption; all the perfect bundles went into *tercios*, large palm bark containers for export.

The small *tabaco del sol* fields around Manicaragua, Camajuani, and Cabaiguan are usually located on slopes for good drainage, and face the morning sun. The fields I saw were free of weeds; the soil surrounding the plants had been cultivated by hand. The sun tobacco varieties produced here are Pelo de Oro and Escambray 70, used as both *capote* leaves and filler. The plants are much shorter than the shade tobacco I'd seen, only about twenty inches high. They have two or three strong branches with a couple of good, bright green cigar leaves on each. These branches are cut at their bases, the

Although Santa Clara is a very old town, its main pedestrian shopping thoroughfare, the Boulevard, is quite modern (*facing page*).

The local cigar factory in the old tobacco town of Remedios features a portrait of José Martí, the legendary leader of the Cuban struggle for independence from Spain in the late nineteenth century.

biggest one first, then the others in subsequent cuttings. The two best leaves from each branch are selected and hung over poles placed on top of notched bamboo posts and left in the field to dry in the sun for three or four days. Then they are carried into the traditional post-and-beam barns. The walls and roofs of the gabled barns are covered by royal palm leaves for good ventilation. The tobacco is eventually shipped to Havana, either to be put into cigars or sent abroad in *tercio* bales.

The best leaves from each branch of the sun grown tobacco are draped over poles on bamboo posts and hung to dry in the field for three or four days at El Marino, a small farm cooperative north of Manicaragua in Las Villas province.

After drying, the sun tobacco leaves are carried into traditional post-and-beam barns that are covered with royal palm leaves for good ventilation (*facing page*).

The Partido

Corrales had urged me to see the different ways of growing wrapper leaves and also the various types of drying barns, so I went to San Antonio de los Banos about ten miles south of Havana. In one of the old town's several plazas, painted houses line one side of the square; on the other side a train from Havana, consisting of a single car, goes by. In the center of the plaza are two monuments. One is old-fashioned, in the style of the Republic: a pillar of white marble with lions at the base, dedicated by Maximo Gomez in 1903. The other is a bronze bust of Antonio Maceo, in the overscaled, heroic style of Social Realism. Both men were successful generals in the War of Independence—and both were cigar smokers.

Early nineteenth-century houses such as this one are typical in the old town of San Antonio de los Banos, where three of the best types of wrapper leaves are grown.

San Antonio de los Banos features several small squares such as this one, which is surrounded by houses and commercial buildings (*facing page*).

The tobacco farms in this area are in pockets of land Cubans call microclimates—oases in the surrounding rocky and less fertile land. Here food crops—cabbage, potatoes, beans, and corn—as well as tobacco are grown. We passed a large experimental agricultural station and a hydroponic farm where lettuce, onions, carrots, tomatoes, radishes, and cabbage are grown in huge corrugated troughs. The soil is a bright, almost unreal red, and has been cultivated right up to the road's edge. Bus-stop shelters, cement fenceposts, and field netting were all stained red where heavy rains mixed with the soil's pigment. Groves of royal palms sometimes separated the cultivated fields. Occasionally, large stone masonry gates and rows of royal palms along the highway designated entrances to the old prerevolutionary plantations. The fields were filled with workers, and trucks and tractors passed us on the highway. I saw a tractor with four young people who looked strong and happy. One of the passengers, a young woman with a cotton scarf tied over her hair, evoked the idealized worker of Soviet propaganda art. As we turned into the Antonio Briones Montoto tobacco farm, named after a Cuban guerilla who died in Venezuela, we could see acres of cloth covering the fields, and a long row of barns. This was clearly a tobacco farm, but the presence of a brigade house and workers dressed in camouflage army fatigues suggested a military outpost. I insisted we pass by the brigade house, knowing that if we stopped there would be indecision and delay, and that permission to visit might not even be granted. We finally stopped at a tobacco barn of the traditional shape, but this barn was covered with a prefabricated sheeting that

Rows of steam-heated curing barns, called *kafrisas*, stand on the Antonio Briones Monto- to collective farm outside San Antonio de los Banos. Tobacco stored in *kafrisas* dries in 21 days versus the drying time of 60 to 80 days in traditional barns.

Cubans call asbestos cement, and had a corrugated tin roofing material. Workers used wooden skids to bring leaves from the fields, instead of the wicker baskets used in the Vuelta Abajo. The skids were just the right width for two men to carry comfortably and to slide through the precast concrete H-shaped posts in the center of the barn.

The brigade members were anxious to show me the best barns. A young woman named Beatriz Cordero asked to guide us. The others took a quick vote of confirmation and we set off on our tour. We drove along a row of barns, stopped, and were introduced to the security guard, Manuel Martínez. The barns looked normal enough until I noticed furnaces at the end of each barn. These barns, called *kafrisas*, are heated by steam. It was a cold day outside, about 48 degrees, but inside it was at least 80 degrees and dark. The center walkway was elevated about three feet and lighted with two 10-watt bulbs. I stood in the middle of the best wrapper leaves (*capa*). The latest leaves to be put in the barn were at my shoulders, and were still green. Above my head were leaves a beautiful shade of light brown, very pale, and even in that dark place they had a glossy sheen. One variety, Connecticut wrapper, was so sheer that I could see my hand through it.

The *jefe de batería* (station chief), Alfredo Santallana, came in. He was young, probably in his late twenties, good-looking, and wore a gold chain with a religious medallion around his neck. Cubans do not use the word "manager," but Santallana is in charge of fifteen *kafrisas* and monitors four technicians and the guard. He studied tobacco for three years at the Juan Tomás Roig school in Havana, a school he said was no longer in existence,

The brigade sign on the Antonio Briones Montoto collective immediately gives the experimental agricultural station and hydroponic farm a quasi-military atmosphere.

Beatriz Cordero, working in one of the curing barns at Antonio Briones Montoto, is one of a group of young workers at the collective who exemplify Cuba's nationalistic ideals (*facing page*).

and has worked in the industry for ten years, eight of these overseeing experimental barns.

The *kafrisas* have been used for eight and a half years in San Antonio de los Banos, and longer in Pinar del Rio. The advantage to using these barns is that the tobacco dries in twenty-one days, whereas in the traditional tobacco barns it takes sixty to eighty days. According to Santallana, the quality of the drying is the same. There is some precedent for heating the barns: in the old style of curing, small wood fires were built to raise the temperature. Alejandro Robaina had told me that on certain occasions he still uses fires to activate curing.

Santallana's work is devoted to producing some of Cuba's finest wrapper leaves. Perhaps because I was standing among so many leaves—at my shoulders, beside my legs, overhead—and since the platform was elevated, I could finally see the differences between the varieties. As I admired the sheerness of the Connecticut wrapper, Santallana winced, saying, "It is too fragile." He feels more secure with the Corojo wrapper leaves that have a little more body. Many smokers feel the same way when the wrapper on the cigar starts to wear away as it is being smoked.

We left the steamy barn and went to a nearby field to see the plants. He was openly critical of the field: "You are not seeing the best." We were looking at a field of Corojo, one of the three wrapper varieties grown in San Antonio. (The others are Connecticut and Havana 92, named for the year it was inaugurated.) On one side of the field, the center and bottom leaves had already been removed. "All you see now is the top, which is always the strongest, and will be used eventually for *tripa* filler, or, if too strong, for cigarettes."

Santallana fired out criticism so forcefully and extensively that it took me by surprise. "Basically," he said, "the problem is a lack of good organization on the part of the cooperative. Most problems are the result of bad timing. The workers are sent a little too late for weeding, for instance, or for tying up the plants."

"But do the workers perform well?" I asked.

"The workers might be okay, but they never arrive quite on time," he replied.

I asked Santallana about his four technicians, whether or not he hires them, and he said that the cooperative sends him his technicians. I asked if he could fire them.

"If one isn't up to standard, I can certainly tell this to the cooperative and get a replacement," he assured me. But the workers go from farm to farm throughout the cooperative, working a few days at a time, sometimes with the plants, other times filling the barn when the leaves are ready, and then moving on. They never work with him more than a few days at a time. This reveals a lot about the Cuban tobacco industry: bureaucracy in the tobacco field is just as aggravating as bureaucracy anywhere else.

Nuria and I left San Antonio de los Banos and went north on the road to Santiago de las Vegas, which, though named for its tobacco fields, no longer produces tobacco. The town does have a monument, however, dedicated to

The curing barns at San Antonio de los Banos are traditional in form, but their cement beams and walls of asbestos sheeting make their construction thoroughly modern.

tobacco farmers and their contribution to Cuban nationalism. On the way, we stopped at the shrine of San Lazaro, a popular shrine where Cubans go on December 17, sometimes on their knees. The church is filled with representations of all of Cuba's most popular saints: the Caridad del Cobre, the Madonna del Regla, St. Martín, and others I didn't recognize. There were purple orchids for San Lazaro, who, Nuria told me, likes the color. She was surprised that Cubans, so short on cash, had bought so many gladioli and dahlias to decorate the altars.

During the following weeks I started to visit the cigar factories, usually accompanied by Nuria but sometimes alone. Now that I knew more about the leaves, I was able to ask about the blends that make up the famous cigars. I also asked the cigar makers where the leaves for their brands came from. Corrales was right: the distinctive flavor of a cigar is the result of blending tobacco varieties from different regions. One thing was certain, *tabaco del sol* is more important to the cigar industry than the cigar treatises suggested, and I had learned to appreciate the role it plays in the complex, sun-filled flavor of a good *habano*.

The Caridad del Cobre, Cuba's patron saint, is one of the many popular religious icons that fill the shrine of San Lazaro on the highway from San Antonio de los Banos to Santiago de las Vegas.

Here, at San Antonio de los Banos, shade tobacco is left to flower to produce seeds. Tobacco in flower symbolizes the continuity of Cuba's great tobacco heritage (*facing page*).

Overleaf: This curing barn for a *tobaco del sol* field near Remedios, still bare of the palm fronds that will cover its frame, reveals Cuba's time-tested construction methods.

José E. Perdomo

LÉXICO
TABACALERO
CUBANO

LA HABANA, CUBA
MCMXL

Nearly every morning for three months I went to the library at the Museum of the City of Havana, crossing the courtyard directly under the gaze of a marble statue of Christopher Columbus. From eight until noon I sat with one eye on the book before me and the other on the courtyard below, where peacocks strolled about, scratching the earth beneath large-leafed plants. Tourists gazed up at the open windows of the library, then at the velvet ropes barricading its stone stairway.

One day the librarian, José Orihuela, had written "tobacco factories" on a slip of paper and placed it in the pages of a large scrapbook to mark an article by Guillermo Herrera, entitled "Monte." The article begins by listing the names and addresses of tobacco warehouses that were situated on Havana's Monte Street in the nineteenth century. "In this part of Monte modest tobacco houses sold loose leaves from just inside their doorways. These were small businesses for private rollers to sell to stores or to customers who preferred a particular *vitola*. They were open to the public, and their doors were right on the street." Herrera continued, "In 1840 there circulated among the *tabacaleros* on Monte a book titled *Cartilla Rústica*, which had a chapter about tobacco. It was simply written, in practical language. All the steps of tobacco growing were explained in a simple narrative between a father and his son. . . . This little book was used by everyone who made a living in tobacco."

After I read Herrera's article I was intrigued by the reference to the *Cartilla Rústica*, which translates as something like "Letters from the Countryside." All the books I'd been reading described the making of the Havana cigar, from field to rolling table, in exactly the same way: they all had the air of a primer. I was eager to find the book that may very well have been the common source of all the others.

I looked in card catalogs all over the city for the *Cartilla Rústica* and didn't find it. Was it simply a legend that one journalist, Guillermo Herrera, passed on in 1940, and printed in the *Police Gazette*? Before leaving Havana I decided to visit the José Martí National Library one last time to look through a few more periodicals, particularly *Revista Tabaco*. The earliest issue the catalog listed was dated 1933; the earliest issue the library had was from 1936, so I placed a request and handed over my passport as security. (The poor state of the national library is a much talked about issue in Cuba. During the recent crisis, which featured fourteen-hour electrical blackouts, the conditions of humidity varied so drastically that people tell of papers that crumbled before their eyes.)

José E. Perdomo's *Léxico Tobacalero Cubano*, an authoritative dictionary of Cuban tobacco published in 1940 (*facing page*), often repeats precisely the information found in *Cartilla Rústica*, a nearly legendary book published in 1840.

Detailed information such as this diagram of a tobacco plant makes the *Léxico* a requisite text for tobacco aficionados (*below*).

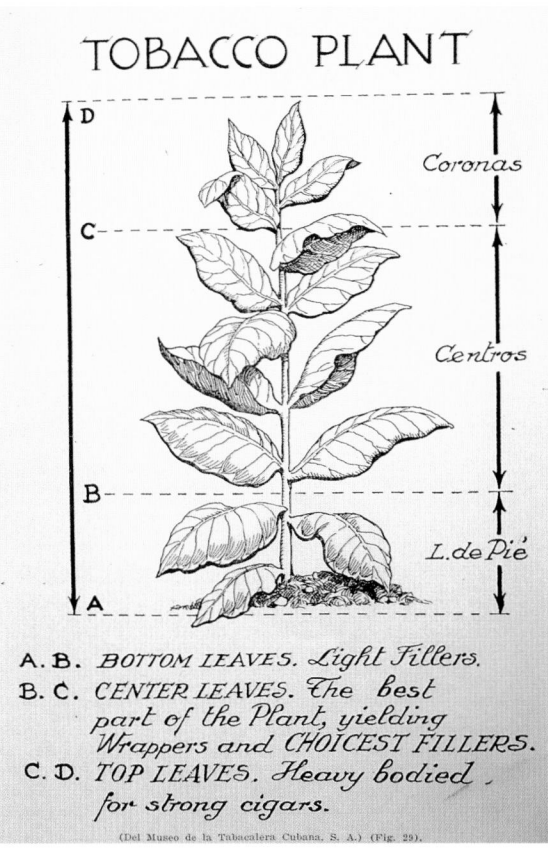

TOBACCO PLANT

D
Coronas
C

Centros

B
L. de Pié
A

A. B. *BOTTOM LEAVES. Light Fillers.*
B. C. *CENTER LEAVES. The best part of the Plant, yielding Wrappers and CHOICEST FILLERS.*
C. D. *TOP LEAVES. Heavy bodied for strong cigars.*

(Del Museo de la Tabacalera Cubana, S. A.) (Fig. 29).

After waiting about twenty minutes, I was at last handed a cardboard folder wrapped with grocer's string. Inside were a couple of issues of *Revista Tabaco*. The January 1938 commemorative issue headlined in English, "1893–1938 Saluting San Juan y Martínez, San Louis [sic], Mecca of Cuban tobacco." The issue contained lesson nine from the *Cartilla Rústica* and confirmed that it was indeed written in 1840, as Guillermo Herrera had described. I'd found it! The set of rules. Lesson nine begins, "Today, Señor, is the day that we had set aside for the lesson about cultivating and the preparation of tobacco, and about some of the tobacco farmers who know the most about raising tobacco on this Island."

VIEW OF THE CALZADA DEL MONTE.

The father then bestows on his son his own personal, somewhat cynical philosophy of tobacco growing. "Tobacco, my son, is like everything else: many mistakes. One uses one's method and nothing much comes from this but fantasy." I've decided that he means you do the best you can, but ultimately it's a puff of smoke. He goes on to say that few farmers have analyzed the processes and methods, or the seasons, that produce tobacco. Therefore, tobacco farmers need to have, in their houses, written instructions about cultivation, so that by conforming to established rules the culture of tobacco may be equal and uniform throughout Cuba.

The selection from the *Cartilla Rústica* began in the front of the magazine, but when I turned to the continuing pages they had been torn out. Still, I was delighted to have found another reference to this book. It seemed that I had read the lines before; the age-old precepts of the Cuban tobacco tradition had been repeated over and over again. I was convinced I'd found a key to the methods Cubans have used to produce the best tobacco in the world for at least a hundred and fifty years.

Six months later I found the *Cartilla Rústica* in English with the help of Virginia Bartow, the Curator of Rare Books at the New York Public Library. She showed me a rare translation by R. C. Wyllie made in 1843. Wyllie had received a copy of the *Cartilla* from Joseph Tucker Crawford, the British consul general in Havana, in January of that year, along with some genuine tobacco seed. The library also holds the original, in Spanish, in the Records of the Patriotic Society of Havana, Volume 12, September 1841.

When I found this translation of the *Cartilla*, it became clear why someone would steal the pages. It is a valuable guide, even for modern farmers, to growing tobacco, and deals with every phase of production—from planting the seeds and recognizing harmful pests, to curing the leaves and packing

In the nineteenth century one of the highest concentrations of tobacco warehouses in Havana was on Monte Street, depicted here in Samuel Hazard's *Cuba with Pen and Pencil*, published in 1874. It was on Monte Street that the *Cartilla Rústica* originally circulated among *tabacaleros*, or tobacco growers.

COMPLETE INSTRUCTION

ON THE

CULTIVATION, PREPARATION, AND PACKING

OF

TOBACCO,

IN THE FORM OF A

DIALOGUE BETWEEN FATHER AND SON.

Translated by Mr. Wyllie, from the Spanish of the Records of the Patriotic Society of Havana, by a permanent Committee thereof, No. 71 of Volumne 12, for September, 1841; received from Joseph Tucker Crawford, Esquire, Her Britannic Majesty's Consul General in Havana, January, 1843, with some genuine Tobacco Seed.

R. C. WYLLIE.

Son. This day, sir, is the day appointed by you to condescend to give me a lesson upon the culture and preparation of tobacco; which, as some judges of territories have informed me, is the most severe branch of agriculture in this Island ; and they that are the most experienced cultivators experience doubts upon the subject at every step.

Cultivator. As to tobacco, my son, there are many errors ; every one has his own method, and hence it is that a small matter is transformed into a bugbear. Few are the farmers who, after judicious meditation, founded on experience, infer that from such and such a process, practised in this or that way, and in this or that season, is produced this or that effect, favorable or unfavorable. The farmers require to have in their houses, an instruction in writing upon that kind of cultivation, so as that by conforming to established rules, the culture of tobacco may be equal and uniform in all its parts.

Son. What kind of land is best for sowing tobacco in ?

Cultivator. The best land for that purpose is where the soil is loose and sandy, dark brownish colour inclining to grey.

Son. On what points ought the fields (for tobacco) to be situated?

Cultivator. The best fields in this Island are situated on the banks of rivers.

Son. In what part of the Islands is the best tobacco produced ?

Cultivator. In the slope below.

Son. What is the cause of that ?

Cultivator. Because the earth is very loose, sandy, fine and dark.

The *Cartilla Rústica,* a dialogue between a father and his son, here in a rare 1843 translation by R. C. Wyllie, is a seminal primer on tobacco cultivation. (Arents Collection, New York Public Library)

them in bundles for market. I began to understand some of the imagery I had seen on labels, as well as the growing practices I had observed in the *vegas*.

I'd traveled in the Vuelta Abajo in August, when the land around the tobacco barns was planted with field corn and the barns were empty of any leaves. It must have been the same in 1840 when the *Cartilla* was written. "In September, after gathering in the crop of the water-maize, you begin to plough the land," the cultivator explains. This is done to "throw down all the weeds, stalks, and other fragments of maize, mixing all these with the earth, so they rot to enrich the soil."

Meanwhile, as I had learned at Alejandro Robaina's farm and by reading José E. Perdomo's 1940 *Léxico Tobacalero Cubano*, the tobacco seeds are sown in the seedbed, generally during the first half of September. In the time of the *Cartilla*, the seeds were planted in nursery gardens surrounded by *canteros*, stone walls high enough to shelter the young plants from strong winds. The father advises his son to "water the seedlings at least every three days, and cover them up with poles and leaves of green plantain to protect them from the heat of the sun during the hours of the day when it is strongest, and also when the rain is heavy. At night they should be left uncovered to receive the dew."

Thirty-five or forty days after planting the seeds, the seedlings are ready to be transplanted in batches over the course of several months, beginning in late October or early November. The *Cartilla* describes the tricky transplanting process: "When you wish to transplant, you pull the seedlings with care, place them in a basket, and carry them to the field after four in the afternoon to avoid the sun, which withers them, and injures them greatly. Many or almost all the farmers leave the plants heaped up in baskets longer than is necessary; and this is bad, because they get heated, and if they take root, they remain backward in growth and do not yield good leaves."

The seedlings are planted about a foot apart in shallow furrows of loose, somewhat dry soil. The *Cartilla* recommends using some system of man-made irrigation, but adds, "without doubt a good season is preferable to all that art can do," so farmers should try to plant in late fall, "when the North winds bring light rains." Five or ten days after transplanting the tobacco, the plants that have died are replaced by others in the second planting. When the weather is ideal, a third of the little plants may die. "There are men so expert," the farmer in the *Cartilla* tells his son, "that of a thousand plants transplanted, they will scarcely lose ten. Therefore, it is not a bad season alone which kills the plants, but also a want of practical skill."

Perdomo's *Léxico*, which mirrors the *Cartilla* exactly in some parts, states that as soon as the plant matures, field workers remove the flower bud from the top. The plant sends out shoots, called suckers, from the stalk, in a natural effort to reproduce itself. The suckers must be removed, so that the nutrients and moisture in the soil are used by the plant to produce larger leaves instead of additional useless stalks. In Cuba nearly everyone has spent some time working in the tobacco fields, and many students spend their Christmas

This antique A-frame curing barn, referred to as a *casa de tabaco*, is still put to good use.

vacations at the "School of the Countryside," removing suckers. I have met art historians, architects, and writers in their forties who remember doing this job, called *deshijar*. Most hated it because the plant is extremely sticky with resin, covering their hands and clothes. In the morning it was cold and claustrophobic inside the netting but by the afternoon it was like a steam room, far too hot for comfort.

When the tobacco plant is mature, leaves are picked one by one, only as each leaf is ready, from the tall, shade grown tobacco plants. After the leaves have been cut, women use huge needles threaded with string to gather the leaves onto lines that are hung over wooden poles called *cujes*. Many women have done this job, either as students or as volunteers during their professional careers. This was one job they liked. They recall the pleasantly cool, shady barns and the friendships made while threading the leaves.

The poles are hung in curing barns while the leaves dry and then ferment. When I visited the tobacco houses, I'd noticed that the poles of leaves were constantly being shifted around in the curing barns, and reading the *Cartilla* I learned why. As soon as the tobacco is brought into the barn, the poles are placed close to one another so that the "pressed" tobacco will heat up slightly and ripen well; it is left like this for three days. On the fourth day, the bars are moved farther apart, allowing the leaves to dry out evenly.

The curing process ends in March when the first showers provide humidity, and when the leaves are sufficiently cured but still moist enough to handle without danger of crumbling. The leaves are then tied into *gavillas*, which look like bouquets of the golden leaves tied at their bases. The *gavillas* are then taken to the grading room.

In the grading room in the Vuelta Abajo I had seen women gently unfolding the leaves and separating the wrapper leaves from the filler leaves. The *Cartilla* describes the sorting process, the *escojida*. Then, each pile of tobacco was covered with plantain leaves instead of burlap or plastic as it is now. "If the tobacco is very dry, it should be covered with green plantain leaves, and if soft and moist, with dry plantain leaves."

Alejandro Robaina examines a *gavilla*, forty or fifty wrapper leaves tied together, as a *tabacalero* would have in 1840 when the *Cartilla Rústica* was first published.

After tobacco leaves have been cut, workers thread them with strings to hang over wooden poles called *cujes* (*facing page*).

The *Cartilla* provides fascinating insight into the various classes of graded tobacco. The names are *injuriado malo, injuriado bueno, desechito,* and *libra.* "Bad injured" tobacco is quality tobacco that has been torn; it is commonly called *tripa*, and is used as filler. It is parcelled into sheaves of forty to fifty leaves tied at their ends with two or three leaves. The "good injured," also of high quality, but with holes in the leaves, is parcelled in the same way. This grade of tobacco will be added to tobacco of less body and quality if the leaves are large and whole. *Desechito* (refuse) is the largest of the best tobacco—very aromatic, with a high cinnamon color and significant body. The *libra* (pound)

grade leaves are shorter, so slightly inferior. When the leaves are judged to be dry enough, both *desechito* and *libra* are tied in parcels of twenty-five leaves. After being parcelled, the tobacco is bundled, then baled and shipped.

Many writers have tried to define why Cuba produces the world's best tobacco. I speculated that it must be the bright red earth I noticed around the two famous tobacco towns, San Juan y Martínez and San Luis, or in San Antonio de los Banos. Yet Robaina's farm had soil of many colors: some of the fields had black soil, other fields were buff-colored with sandy soil, and the fields near his house were a combination of red clay and sand, with a good many pebbles. The little bible of the cigar industry has some answers. The son asks, "What kind of land is best for tobacco?" The father replies: loose and sandy, dark brown to grey. "Where ought the fields be situated?" The best fields on the island are situated along the rivers, the father tells him, especially the San Juan y Martínez, Cuyaguateje, and Hondo. And the tobacco that is not grown on the banks of rivers? According to the *Cartilla,* the fields of red soil yield tobacco leaves that are large, strong, and not very good-tasting. This tobacco, nevertheless, keeps for much longer than any other varieties.

Echoing what Raul Corrales had stressed about the importance of sun tobacco and what Esther Luisa Hernandez had told me about her blends of filler leaves, the father in the *Cartilla* displays a slight contempt for growers who insist on producing only the beautiful but mild wrapper leaves. "In almost all parts of the world, the tobacco of this Island has a high value. The North Americans pay well for the yellow tobacco. . . . Every means used to make tobacco yellow, which is not so naturally, injures its strength and its quality. Every farmer ought to content himself with the class of tobacco his land produces." The father urges, "Let him make his tobacco burn well and improve its flavor, and not destroy its strength, if it be of good quality, merely with the idea of giving it the color which caprice has made fashionable." Pale tobacco still drives the market 150 years later, but I have come to understand that there is much more to the best *habanos* than even the most elegant outer wrappers suggest.

The partially exposed frame of this curing barn at the El Marino cooperative shows in detail the simple materials that continue to be used today.

Overleaf: The Malecón, which literally means "seawall," has been Havana's hub of activity since Old Havana's earliest days.

ROLLED BY HAND

This H. Upmann box, dating from 1920, features a picture of the H. Upmann factory, built around 1890. (Collection: Tobacco Museum, Havana)

EARLY CIGAR MAKING AND THE CITY

"Cheap Cigar Factory," an illustration in Samuel Hazard's charming book *Cuba with Pen and Pencil* (1871), shows what was probably a typical cigar factory in the nineteenth century. Open doors reveal eight people, including a Chinese man with a single pigtail and a woman with a long skirt among the male cigar rollers. The factory owner sits behind a grilled window, wearing a coat and smoking a cigar. A sign, *Fabricas de Tabacos*, is displayed on front of the building, and little signs designating *Tabacos Puros* and *Vuelta Abajo* are on the walls. *Puros* was a name given to cigars to distinguish them from cigarettes. (In the United States it has acquired a different meaning: pure Havana tobacco, unblended and undiluted with foreign tobacco.) *Vuelta Abajo*, of course, refers to the famous tobacco-growing region.

Among the books the librarian at the Havana Museum of the City gave me were old city directories. From these I was able to make a list of the more than two hundred *tabaquerías* (tobacco businesses) operating in 1840. In the directory compiled by Eduardo Jones, each business is designated "c" for *comerciante*, which were probably sellers of tobacco leaves, or "f" for *fabricante*, a small tobacco factory where cigars and cigarettes were hand rolled. Occasionally "alm. tab." is noted, meaning *almacen de tabaco*, a warehouse.

Using these directories, and a map published around the same time by Antonio Maria de La Torre, which had the house numbers on all the streets in Havana, it was easy to see where cigars were being rolled, stored, and sold. *Tabaquerías* were scattered throughout the city, and cigars were

This map of Havana by José Maria de la Torre, published in 1857, includes the street numbers of each building. To the right, the outlines of the walls of the old city still appear.
(Collection: New York Public Library)

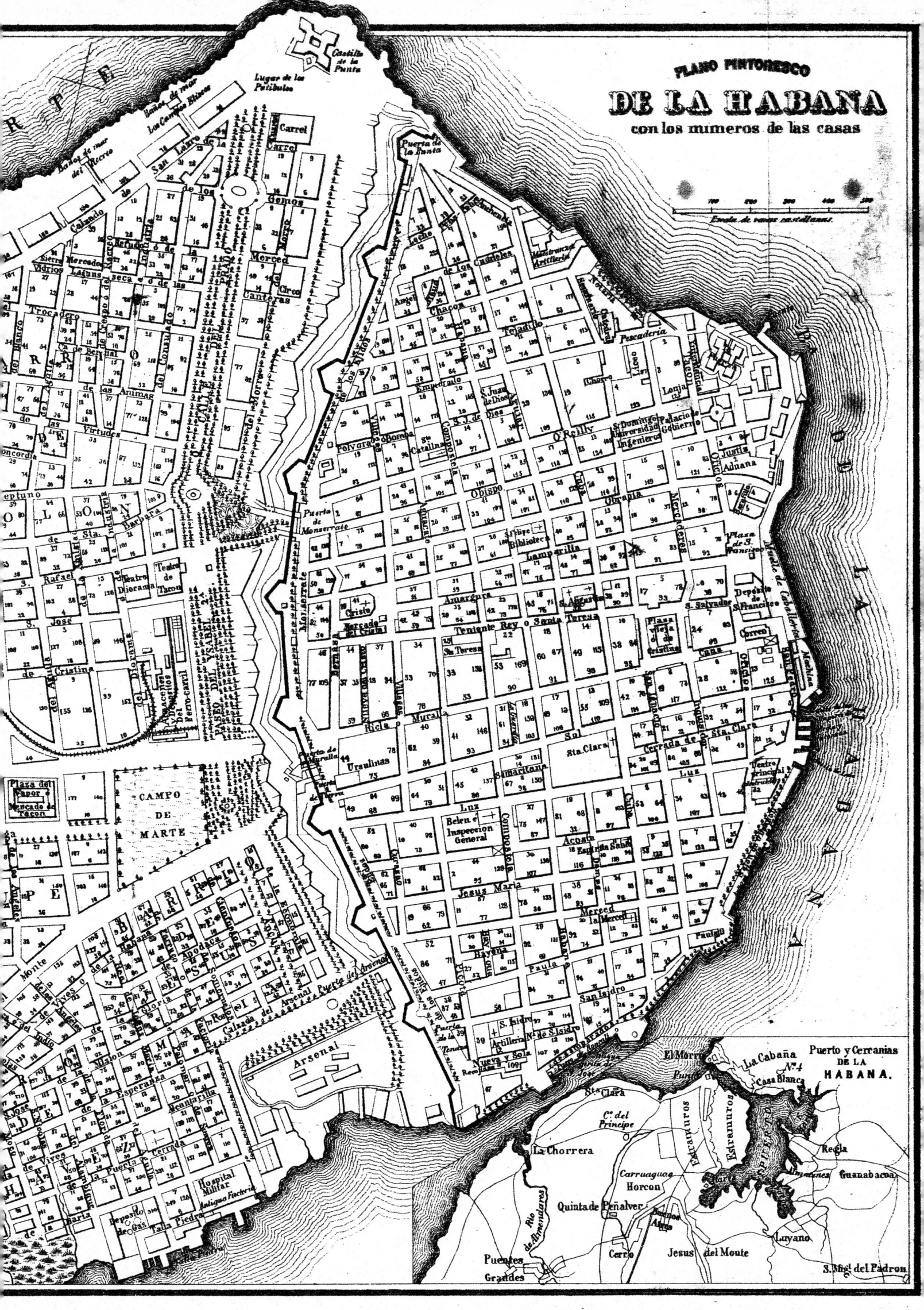

PLANO PINTORESCO
DE LA HABANA
con los numeros de las casas

Escala de varas castellanas.

Puerto y Cercanias
DE LA
HABANA.

being manufactured everywhere. I began to understand why tobacco and cigars soon became synonymous with the city and why cigars are called, quite appropriately, Havanas. A large number of the businesses were located inside the old walled city, now referred to as Old Havana, on the streets named Obispo, Sol, Teniente Rey, Bernaza, Habana, Gloria, and Compostella. The buildings on these streets, mostly one- and two-story houses, have changed very little. They are now churches, shops, and houses, but once they were small cigar factories. The house numbers have changed since the de La Torre map was published, but the locations are the same and still easy to establish.

In the early days of tobacco manufacturing, workers rolled cigars in their homes to supplement other employment, or, as in Hazard's illustration, in workrooms where a group of people rolled together. The owner would buy tobacco from one of the wholesale houses, choosing the blend of leaves and consistency of color that he preferred. After the cigars were rolled, bundles were taken to the export traders and sorted by size and probably by color, and exported under the dealer's name. Thus, when Jaime Partagás founded his label in 1843, he probably traveled around Havana, buying cigars from houses on Monte, Obispo, or Concordia, or the rollers came to his establishment at One Cristina Street. The exporter sold cigars under his own special trademark, printed on small labels attached to the packing cases shipped from the port of Havana. The label carried a trade name or the exporter's name, and always the Havana street address where his business was located. The exporters had several brands to offer the buyers, and, after a while, some brands were preferred by foreign customers more than others.

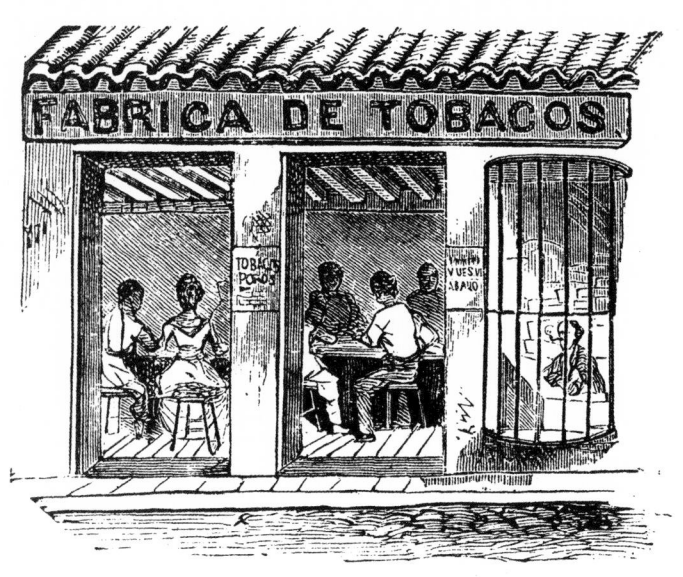

Samuel Hazard's illustration entitled "Cheap Cigar Factory," from his *Cuba with Pen and Pencil,* depicts a typical nineteenth-century cigar factory.

The next commercial directory of Havana, issued in 1859, lists names and addresses of factory owners as well as the brands they sold. According to the directory, there were 688 brands of cigars and cigarettes rolled in Havana. During this period, from around 1840 until 1875, the great names of the modern Havana cigar industry began to appear—Julian Alvarez y Hermanos, at San Nicolas 120 (Henry Clay, Flor de Henry Clay, Franck Pierce, and Diana); Antonio Cabarga, at Calzada de Galiano 25 (La Corona, an ancestor of the present La Corona factory); Antonio Caruncho, at 104 Campanario (Intimidad and Super Omnia); Larrañaga, at 46 San Miguel (Por Larrañaga, which was to become the cigar of style in the 1920s); and Jaime Partagás and H. Upmann.

The 1859 directory lists only three "first-class" factories—those employing more than fifty people. One was Cabañas, established by Francisco Cabañas in 1797, considered to be the oldest cigar factory. Another was owned by Vicente Martínez Ybor, who later established the cigar industry in Tampa, Florida. The third was the factory of José de Cabarga and Company.

By the time H. E. Heinen published his directory in 1873, there were ten tobacco factories employing more than fifty people: Julian Alvarez; G. Bock and Co.; Antonio Caruncho; José Castillo and Suarez; Diaz, Bances and Co.; Anselmo Gonzalez del Valle (Cabañas); José Partagás; Juan F. Perez del Rio; Juan B. Romero; and H. Upmann. According to Samuel Hazard, who visited the Cabañas factory, it employed over five hundred operators, all male.

At this time there were only sixty-five small factories left in the city. On the other hand, there were sixty-five tobacco warehouses for *tabaco en rama*, wholesale leaf tobacco. Nearly all of these warehouses were located on Monte Street. On the de La Torre map, Monte Street was the city terminus of the old highway leading to Havana from the tobacco fields. In the eighteenth century it was the main road from the tobacco fields of Bejucal, San Antonio de los Banos, and the Vuelta Abajo. Today it has been renamed Maximo Gomez, but it is still the major street south, lined with somewhat dilapidated buildings and known to all *Habaneros* simply as Monte.

The city of Havana changed at the end of the nineteenth century. Architect Carlos Venegas has written about how the walls that surrounded the old part of the city were demolished and the wide swath of land that curves behind the old walled city was redeveloped. In the ditches where the old walls had been were installed wide boulevards, parks, and monumental buildings linking the two cities—Habana Vieja, composed of cramped, overcrowded streets, and Centro Habana, with its rows of early nineteenth-century houses.

Tobacco factories played a key role in the urban development plan, which called for buildings of great stature and importance. Partagás, La Corona, José Gener, and Calixto López responded by constructing grand tobacco factories designed to look like palaces. In her *Guide to Colonial Havana,* Maria Elena Martín writes that in the age of the tobacco industry—from the late 1800s—these new factories were characterized by their unified exteriors and interiors decorated with costly materials. Partagás and La Corona still actively produce export cigars in their original factories, the Gener building is now a printing plant and is a ghost of its former glory, and the Calixto López factory produces domestic cigars. The H. Upmann factory is located in this area, having moved into the old Carvajal factory in the 1940s.

Hidden in Centro Habana, the Romeo y Julieta factory most closely resembles the ideal cigar factory of the late 1800s. The Rey del Mundo factory is located directly behind Romeo y Julieta. The Por Larrañaga factory is closed, but is used as a tobacco storehouse. The Menéndez García factory is now a warehouse. The old Lobeto building stands, but is closed; much of the former warehouse district still exists around Monte Street.

A relatively new factory in the suburbs, producing the Cohiba, has become the headquarters of the most stylish brand. In addition, the Heroes del Moncada factory in Marianao, a remote part of the city, produces export cigars, and Las Mambisas, in Guanabacoa, has a few top rollers who are making a small number of cigars for export which are sent to the Rey del Mundo factory.

FAMOUS FACTORIES TODAY

Partagás
Established 1843
Formerly known as Ramón Cifuentes, 1900
currently Francisco Pérez German
Industria No. 520 (between Dragones and Barcelona)
Habana Vieja

At the edge of the Parque de la Fraternidad near Monte, at the foot of the Capitol Building, is the Partagás factory. The main building is four stories capped by a *remate superior,* a roofline of baroque curves topped by the urns that grace many urban Spanish buildings, especially churches. The *remate superior* is a finishing touch and a sort of billboard for the name of the establishment. "1845" is carved in the facade, designating the founding of Partagás, although the accepted date is 1843. (The building was constructed at the end of the nineteenth century.) Inside the palace is an interior patio surrounded by colored glass windows, imitating important urban residences in the city. The exterior is painted in old-fashioned Victorian colors: cream walls and chocolate brown detailing.

The Partagás factory is located behind the Capitol building, now the Academy of Sciences Library, in Old Havana (*facing page*).

The plaque at the entrance of the Partagás factory commemorates Ramón Cifuentes's ownership of the factory at the turn of the century. The factory is now state owned and named Francisco Pérez German.

Partagás was later sold to a Spaniard, Ramón Cifuentes, as the plaque by the door states, and the factory's latest renovation appears to have been in the 1940s. The huge interior rooms have been divided into smaller spaces by trellis walls, a kind of garden scheme that recalls department stores of that period. The postrevolutionary name of the factory is Francisco P. German.

Outside the building, I looked at the balconies along the front of the building. All the *vanos*—full-length sets of windows, shutters, and doors—were open, and cigar rollers were taking a break in the fresh air and bright sunshine. The building gives the impression that something fun and social is happening within. There are four hundred employees of whom more than half are rollers.

Jaime Partagás was a great salesman, making the brand of his cigars famous in London from the very beginning. William Gill wrote that Partagás was "a past grand-master in the art of tobacco confection." Although no one knows who was the first to use the decorated box, Jaime Partagás is one of the contenders. The image of his cigars has always been one of elegance, and the Partagás label featured the eternal woman to portray this elegance. A crowned female is in the center, sitting on a throne. Two goddesses stand on either side of her: Industry, with a wheel at her feet and hammer in hand, and Art, who holds a palette of oil paints. Gold medals from the Paris Competitions of 1867 through 1879 and 1889 are at their feet.

The factory's cigar store, though it is not managed by Partagás but by the state export industry, is probably the most visited in Havana. It is located inside the factory and is dark and cool, with a bar at one end. There one can sit down on a comfortable bar stool, order one of the three standard drinks of Cuba—rum, Coca-Cola, or coffee—and smoke a Montecristo from the glass humidor on the bar. Luis Lara, a dapper Spaniard who works at Partagás, was in the cigar store one day, and I asked him about smoking in Havana. He has smoked three to six cigars a day for forty-two years. I watched as he drew a little silver cutter from his pocket, cut his cigar, and lighted it with a cedar stick.

"Every box of Havana cigars is packaged with a thin sheet of cedar between the layers," he said, tearing one of them into strips, and even opening one of the metal tubes to carefully twist and remove a little sheet of cedar to show me. Cubans are convinced that it is the one wood that preserves the cigar.

The store at the Partagás factory, which is probably the most visited in Havana, features a bar where one can order any of Cuba's three standard drinks—rum, Coca-Cola, or coffee—with one's cigar.

"Use these little sticks to light the cigar and you will not contaminate the flavor of the aroma." He is right: there is no smell of matches to conflict with the initial tobacco aroma. Though I rarely saw people using them (since most Cubans do not have access to boxed and exported cigars), many smokers made a point of showing me their cedar matches bought specially for lighting cigars.

Lara has the entire industry at his disposal. What does he smoke? "Well, I start the day with a light, sweet cigar and then make a selection in the middle of the day based on whether or not I am lunching for business or lunching normally." He told me that every situation requires a different cigar. I asked him to explain.

"I breakfast at eight with coffee and a Cohiba panatela, joyita, or margarita. Usually I have another coffee, at ten or eleven—the way people do in Cuba—with a Cohiba exquisito or something similar." I think about all the people who would love to start their day with two Cohibas.

"With a normal lunch," he continued, "around one o'clock, I have a Petit Punch, a Montecristo No. 4, or a Romeo y Julieta No. 2 De Luxe." He explained, "These last about forty-five minutes, but if I'm having a business lunch, say around one-thirty, which I expect to last until three, I smoke a Churchill by Romeo y Julieta, Punch, Hoyo de Monterrey, or a Partagás De Luxe, which last about one and a half hours."

I had been counting the cigars by making little marks in my notebook. "Go on, tell me more," I coaxed. Lara is a big man with white hair, a trim, athletic figure, and an easy smile. He laughed. "A big lunch, which could go

This Partagás label from 1920 features the goddesses Industry and Art at either side of an "eternal" woman, all of which conveys an enduring image of grandeur. (Collection: Alberto Bustamante)

on until four o'clock, would require a Double Corona (two hours smoke), Punch, Hoyo de Monterrey, or Lusitania.

"For dinner at eight, with coffee arriving around nine-fifteen" (he called this a "strong" dinner of beef and red wine), "I would smoke a Partagás No. 8. Then around ten or eleven with coffee and cognac, I like to smoke a Médaille d'Or No. 2."

I counted six marks in my notebook: breakfast, coffee, lunch, dinner, coffee, coffee. We continued to smoke our cigars and watched the shoppers from South America, Europe, and Asia as they selected boxes of cigars from the glass cases in the shop.

I asked Lara if he really smokes like this or was this regime a sort of primer for cigar smoking. He answered that he has always varied his *vitolas*. "You get up each morning and smoke how you feel," he said, admitting that he is asthmatic.

H. Upmann
Established 1844
Currently known as José Martí
Amistad No. 407 (between Dragones and Barcelona)
Habana Vieja

Around 1944, a hundred years after it was founded by Herman Upmann, the H. Upmann Factory moved to the street behind the Partagás factory to a building site that once housed the Carvajal cigar factory. The name of the factory is now José Martí, but the H. Upmann sign still hangs outside the building.

H. Upmann had two factories, one at 159 Carlos III, built around 1890. The brand was also produced at the Menéndez García factory at 609 Virtudes, a charming building that is now a warehouse of export tobacco.

Herman Upmann's cigars received medals in Paris (1855 and 1867), London (1862), Oporto (1866), Moscow (1872), Vienna (1873), Chicago (1893), Amsterdam (1894), Sydney (1905), and Liege (1907). In the beginning of the century, Upmann's "yearly output of cigars was by far the largest of any factory in Havana," according to William Gill.

Today the government assigns to certain factories the job of producing particular brands. The H. Upmann factory rolls some of Cuba's most prestigious cigars: the entire line of Montecristos and Cohiba's large cigars—esplendidos, the largest of the siglos, and the robustos. They also produce, of course, H. Upmann.

At H. Upmann, I asked to see the leaves that were being blended that day to make the Montecristo No. 1 (double corona) cigar. The old Spanish blender unfolded a wrapper of thick plastic which contained the ingredients. That day I discovered an interesting point about the blend: only the big cigars—for instance, the Montecristo Nos. 1 through 4—contain all three filler leaves. Until then I had assumed that every cigar is composed of three types of filler leaves—*ligero, volado,* and *seco*—and two additional leaves to package the cigar, the *capote* and *capa.* I began to realize that small cigars, which make up so many export sizes, are just two leaves, *volado* and *capa.* I'd certainly watched plenty of small panatelas being rolled, but hadn't watched closely enough. I now asked the blender to show me the exact leaves, just to be sure I understood. He seemed to be charmed by my discovery, treating me like an ingenue lost in a tobacco factory. He produced the *volado.* This is the essential combustion leaf, which makes the cigar burn. Since it is generally accepted that the outer binder and wrapper leaves have no real flavor, all the flavor of a small cigar is in one

In this box of H. Upmann coronas major manufactured in 1940 is a product with a legacy of international gold medals (*below*). (Collection: Tobacco Museum, Havana)

H. Upmann has occupied this factory in Old Havana since around 1944. The name of the factory is now officially José Martí, but the H. Upmann sign still hangs outside (*facing page*).

25 - CORONAS MAJOR - 25

96

In the leaf preparation room at the H. Upmann factory (*above and right*) leaves are blended in various combinations to conform to the standards of each brand.

variety of leaf. So, if you are smoking a Montecristo No. 5, for example, that leaf had better be full of flavor. The tobacco for these cigars is grown in the sun, *tabaco del sol*, in the manner explained precisely in the *Cartilla Rústica*.

Since we were in the blender's department, I asked to see the best *capa*. The leaves were moist in their large wooden boxes lined with thick black plastic and gently covered with damp burlap. The sides of the boxes were marked with numbers rating the quality. The blender and his assistant looked at all the boxes in the room, consulted their slips of paper, and drew out the best leaves. They presented me with a bouquet of leaves that were like tissue paper, glossy, and all exactly the same size and color. I asked what cigars these leaves would cover that day. They glanced at the order form and told me

Montecristo No. 1. As we left the room I asked to see the *capa* leaves that would be used to roll the Cohiba esplendidos. The blender took me to the cashier—or at least she looked like a cashier in a booth with a window—where the rollers apply for leaves. She looked at her orders and drew out a package of folded Cohiba wrapper leaves. They were toffee-colored, large, soft, glossy, the same weight as a Hermès scarf, but much more transparent.

I asked to see the cabinet, a large, walk-in vault which I privately call "the bank." There were two thousand cigars in bundles, and boxes and boxes of *capa*, their most valuable commodity, all stored in blond wooden boxes from the 1940s.

The cabinet, a large, walk-in vault, at H. Upmann contains thousands of cigars and boxes of *capa* leaves.

El Rey del Mundo
Established 1848
Formerly known as Díaz Brothers, Cuesta Rey & Co.
Currently Carlos Balino
San Carlos No. 816, Centro Habana

Behind the Romeo y Julieta factory stands the small Rey del Mundo factory. (Rey del Mundo cigars were once rolled at 852 Padre Varela; the labels still carry that address.) The Carlos Balino factory, named after a turn-of-the-century union reformer, has a vertical layout with departments on three floors. I arrived at ten o'clock, just when the workers were finishing their milky coffee and cheese sandwiches supplied by the factory on morning break. I briefly stepped inside the infirmary and watched as a worker had her blood pressure checked—a serious concern in an occupation in which everyone touches and inhales nicotine all day. Over the loudspeakers I heard the voice of the reader, reading the daily news.

Reading for the workers in cigar factories is an institution that has existed for well over a century. The factory workers audition readers and hire them based on their reputation and the list of books that he or she reads best. Like clockwork, in every cigar factory the reader begins at eight. First the reader reads from *Granma*, the government newspaper, and from ten to a quarter past eleven does the same while conducting a discussion of current events. After lunch until a quarter past two, the factory workers listen to a novel. In a sense, the morning news—call it nonfiction or even propaganda, depending on your point of view—is an opener for the feature act, *la novela*.

Novels have been read aloud in cigar factories since about 1865. Some novels that show up every ten years or so are *Les Misérables, Cecilia Valdes,* and *Don Quijote de la Mancha.* My friend, architect Mario Coyula, said, "In Cuba before the Revolution, men who were completely illiterate knew the classics, the plays of Shakespeare, and most modern novels. And even though they could not read or write, they were well versed in current political issues."

The Rey del Mundo factory, officially called Carlos Balino after a turn-of-the-century union reformer, features a vertical layout around a central court (*facing page*).

Though labels evolve over time, many elements often remain: the group of children on an antique Rey del Mundo label (*top*) and the menagerie pulling the chariot on the current label (*bottom*) both represent the major continents. (Collection: Alberto Bustamante)

Romeo y Julieta
Established 1875
Currently known as Antonio Briones Montoto
Padre Varela No. 852 (Belascoain), Centro Habana

Carlos III and Padre Varela streets intersect at a colonial stone house, now converted into a school, with a beautiful street arcade and lacy iron grillwork on the doors and windows. From this point Padre Varela Street runs downhill, and you enter a part of Havana that seems to be unchanged by the twentieth century. Four blocks down the street is the Romeo y Julieta factory. Its presence can be felt immediately. The building was painted hot sienna with chocolate-colored masonry around the windows when I visited in January, but by September it had been bleached by the sun to a conservative pale brown. This three-story building now houses the Antonio Briones Montoto cigar factory, where the major house brand is Romeo y Julieta, though Quai d'Orsay, Rey del Mundo, San Luis Rey, Sancho Panza, Gispert, Rafaël Gonzales, and the new Cuaba are also rolled there. The arcade floor, raised a few steps above the street, is a patterned tile that contrasts with the dirty cement sidewalk. "Cuesta Rey & Co. 1914" is carved in the facade. (The original Romeo y Julieta factory at 2 Padre Varela Street is a gutted-out shell.) There are ironwork balconies along the second and third floors painted a bright, shiny black.

The entire first floor facade seems to be open to the street, except for a little wooden barricade and the ever-present concierge to stop you. These women are tougher than the civil guard nearby, in his green khakis with a tie-on red armband and pistol around his waist. The effect is that the building seems off-limits, but not sinister. The factory's long, open lobby is beautiful: green glazed tiles cover the walls, and an iron staircase curves gracefully up toward the ceiling, which has classical moulding with laurel wreaths painted pink and green.

Segundo Delgado, Director of Production at the Romeo y Julieta factory, has a somewhat gnarled face, deeply lined but not old, and wears a crew cut. (This 1950s look suits Havana. The young waiters at the bohemian Cafe de Paris wear their hair this way.) Delgado is a classic Havana man, and accepted me very graciously at his off-limits-to-nearly-everybody cigar factory, arranging for me to meet the famous roller, Esther Luisa Hernandez. As we walked to the back of the lobby, behind the big iron staircase, we passed a temporary beauty parlor. Any woman in the factory who wanted her hair cut or shampooed and set could do so that day. I'd glimpsed the camaraderie in

MADE IN HABANA, CUBA

The Romeo y Julieta label is particularly successful at conveying the discriminating gentleman's ardent relationship with his cigars.

Though the first floor loggia of the former Romeo y Julieta factory in Central Havana, officially called Antonio Briones Montoto, seems to invite passers-by, the stern female concierges make sure the factory is kept off-limits to nearly everyone (*facing page*).

the cafeterias at other cigar factories, but this was the first time I had seen an example of the reputed family atmosphere. In a cigar factory, nearly everyone has been born into tobacco families. Fathers, mothers, often a sister or brother work in the factory and secure jobs for their children as they mature. Delgado had just told me that he had begun working when he was eleven years old with his father, a *tabacalero,* and now his son is a department chief and his brother works in leaf selection.

All the big, turn-of-the-century cigar factories have similar floor plans. Romeo y Julieta, like the other factories in Havana, is divided into departments. The leaf is handled on the ground floor, while stemming, sorting, rolling, box decorating, and ringing are on upper floors. Rolling takes place in a long, open room called a gallery.

Romeo y Julieta was founded in 1875 by Inocencia Alvarez. Its label symbolism is one of the most successful in the business, since Romeo is a character given over to a love affair, however ill-fated. This sentiment has always been the myth of a gentleman's relationship to cigars. The label shows Romeo, the man committed to romance at all costs, climbing up a ladder to visit Juliet, daughter of the opposing clan. The picture has changed almost imperceptibly over the years: Juliet has been a brunette, a redhead, and a blonde; Romeo once wore a long knife, which looked more like a sheathed machete, on his belt, but it has been shortened over time. There is a large tapestry draped over the balcony, cushioning Romeo's ladder. Cuban filmmaker Tomás Gutierrez Alea, in his short *The Art of the Cigar,* framed the label in a diagonal close-up. For a moment it appears that the two lovers have finally consummated their affair and Romeo is sprawling on Juliet's counterpane.

The quality of the Romeo y Julieta cigar has always been excellent. Gold medals soon joined the couple. In 1910 the factory received the highest recognition at all the international expositions. Winston Churchill smoked a big Romeo y Julieta, creating a silhouette eternally associated with the double corona, and in turn the factory named them Churchills.

In December of 1996, the Romeo y Julieta factory launched a lovely little cigar with an Indian name, the Cuaba. The shape is old-fashioned, slim at the end and fat in the middle. The factory produces it in four sizes: generoso, favorito, bouquet, and petit bouquet. The smallest one is reminiscent of the *cicadas,* the old Spanish *cigarros,* that gave *habanos* their popular name. Cuaba is the word for an Indian torch, a piece of wood that the Taino Indians used to light their way at night, or to illuminate their houses. It is an easy word to say in any language, and suggests the cigar's country of origin.

The long, open lobby at the Romeo y Julieta factory features beautiful glazed tiles and graceful mouldings (*facing page*).

The Romeo y Julieta factory produces a wide variety of brands including Quai d'Orsay, Gispert, and the new Cuaba in addition to the major house brand, Romeo y Julieta.

The former Corona factory, across from the Presidential Palace, now the Museum of the Revolution in Old Havana, is currently the Miguel Fernandez Roig factory, although it is still called La Corona.

La Corona
Established 1888
Currently known as Miguel Fernandez Roig
Open to the public
Zulueta No. 106, Habana Vieja

The architecture of these grand factories provides us with a metaphor for the state of the Havana cigar industry at the end of the nineteenth century. These beautiful facades acted as false fronts for a sinking industry.

In 1888, the British purchased two important properties: Partagás and Henry Clay and Bock. In 1896, Havana Cigar and Tobacco Factories, a London company, was established. They held the controlling interest in thirty-five cigar factories, La Corona and La Legitimidad among them. In 1899, the Havana Commercial Company, a New York company, bought twelve cigar factories in Havana and merged them with García Bros. and Company, who sold leaf tobacco. This company facilitated the acquisition of Havana's tobacco industry by the American Tobacco Company. In 1902, ATC absorbed the Havana Commercial Company and eventually acquired the capital stock in two important factories, the Marques de Pinar del Rio and Hija de Cabañas y Carvajal. Henry Clay and Bock and the thirty-five factories under Havana Cigar and Tobacco Factories remained officially registered British companies but financial control passed to ATC. Cuban Land and Leaf Tobacco Company, a subsidiary of ATC, was established from the lands belonging to Henry Clay and Cabañas y Carvajal, with fields outside San Juan y Martínez providing a guaranteed supply of high quality Vuelta Abajo leaf tobacco.

Historian Jean Stubbs describes how the prosperous Havana export cigar industry was destroyed by U.S. protectionism. The McKinley Tariff Law of 1890 increased duties from $2.50 to $4.50 per pound on cigars imported into the United States, maintaining a 25 percent *ad valorem*. According to Stubbs, "It has been calculated that on 1,000 cigars, weighing 14 pounds and valued at 80 pesos, 83 pesos were paid in customs duties and internal taxes. The result of this was that yet more manufacturers emigrated and, importing the Cuban leaf, began to consolidate their position in the manufacturing world of the United States." In the 1890s a new area of tobacco manufacturing was established in Tampa, Florida, where quality cigars were produced by Cuban rollers from imported Cuban leaf. The bottom line was this: cigars rolled with Cuban leaf and made abroad were cheaper than those manufactured and exported from Havana.

An important factor was the War of Independence led by José Martí from 1895 to 1898. In the east, some of the tobacco fields of Yara and Bayamo were battlefields. To the west, major tobacco producing families of Pinar del Rio left Cuba to establish tobacco plantations in Tampa. Ybor City, for example, grew up around the factory of Vicente Martínez Ybor. The families in Florida were still closely tied to Cuba and supporters of independence. Donations for Martí

were raised by these families—and by cigar rollers in particular, many of whom returned to Cuba after the United States occupation of Cuba (1898 to 1902) ended and the independent Cuban Republic was formed.

The American Tobacco Company built a palace of three stories at 106 Agramonte, also known as Zulueta Street. The building is situated in the shadow of the Presidential Palace. Apparently the building was nicknamed El Panteon, a name usually given to cemeteries, for all the old cigar companies buried there. Today it is the Miguel Fernandez Roig cigar factory, but is still commonly referred to and carries the sign of La Corona.

The cigar manufacturers' union and the tobacco growers' union started trade relations with the United States which resulted in the Reciprocal Trade Treaty of 1903. Cuba opened her doors to American imports in return for tobacco and sugar exports, Cuba's two major industries. The problem was, from the Cuban point of view, that the United States continued to import quality leaf tobacco but very few cigars. The industry fought back. There developed a group of independent cigar factories in fierce competition with the ATC group. Some of these had Spanish capital backing. Ramón Cifuentes bought Partagás in 1900, Ramón Arguelles acquired Romeo y Julieta in 1903, and Estaquio Alonso directed Por Larrañaga, making gains with export cigars and domestic sales. Several writers have noted that London cigar buyers remained constant in their love of Havanas and were especially important clients during this period. Partagás and Gener stayed afloat by moving into cigarette production, as did Calixto López and Rodriguez Menéndez. Although the industry never regained its mid-nineteenth-century prominence, sales increased after World War I into the 1920s. The Depression and machine-rolled cigars brought hard times to Tampa as well as Havana. It was not until the 1950s that cigar smoking became stylish again, and the demand for quality Havana cigars was as great as it was in the 1920s.

Cigar rollers have played major roles in decisive events in the history of modern Cuba: their donations to José Martí facilitated the formation of an independent Cuban republic.

Overleaf: In the leaf preparation room workers organize leaves into manageable stacks for the blenders, sorters, and rollers.

Heroes del Moncada
Established circa 1952
Calle 57 No. 13402, Marianao

Marianao is an old village which is now part of the city of Havana. The Heroes del Moncada is a modestly sized factory with a large rolling room on the upper story; the other departments are on the ground floor where all the major brands of export cigars are rolled, boxed, and shipped. They also make a small number of national cigars, including very good-looking brevas made of blond tobacco (called *Pita*). I was told that this factory did not originate in Havana, but was moved from Las Villas Province in 1952 by its owner, José Ramón Piedra.

    I arrived before lunch, after the reading of the news, and was met by the Communist Party Secretary, the Union Secretary, the Human Resources Manager, the Director of Production, and the Director, in that order. My arrival delayed one of the major events of the day, the reading of the production report to the rollers. Since the factory is trying to increase its production by three percent, each roller's name and the percentage of their production goal they have achieved is read over the loudspeaker. There were not many rollers in the gallery, but Cuba's goal is to roll 100,000,000 cigars, and the rollers at Heroes del Moncada intend to do their part.

Now located in Marinao, a section of Havana that was once an old village, the Heroes del Moncada cigar factory produces all the major brands of export cigars (*facing page*).

The boxing department at Heroes del Moncada occupies the building's ground floor with other support departments, while a large rolling room occupies the entire second floor (*below*).

Overleaf: In the color selection department at Heroes del Moncada, workers carefully sort cigars below a poster of the popular salsa group Los Van Van.

Las Mambisas
Date unknown
Estrada Palma No. 103, Guanabacoa

At the tiny Las Mambisas factory at 103 Estrada Palma Street in Guanabacoa, a few of the factory's oldest and best cigar rollers were making export
cigars for the *patria,* the country, which are contributed to the Carlos Balino
factory (El Rey del Mundo) to help in the nationwide push to roll more
habanos. A careful allotment of leaves from San Juan y Martínez and San
Luis in the Vuelta Abajo were in the corner of the office at Las Mambisas for
these great cigars.

The *habanos* at the tiny factory for Las Mambisas in Guanabacoa, Havana are stored in a
small cabinet.

Las Mambisas employs its oldest and best
rollers for its export cigars (*facing page*).

El Laguito
Established 1966
Avenida 146 No. 2302, Cubanacan, Playa

The Cohiba factory is a house, more properly a villa, in a part of the city near the famous old country club. Unlike other factories (most of which are named for heroes of the Revolution), this one takes its name from a section of the city, El Laguito, which was, in the old days, the most glamorous. For years the factory was where Fidel's personal cigars were rolled for his own use and as gifts to statesmen. At the factory there is a very simple plywood cigar cabinet where Fidel's cigars were stored; they opened it for me after hunting down the keys. It was nearly empty. One shelf had a few loose cigars in a cloth strip that originally held a bundle. Fidel has not smoked in over ten years, and since the Cohiba blend has come to represent Cuba's best cigars, there is no need for Fidel to hand out cigars. Now the factory produces these special gifts for the entire cigar world.

Women had always been part of the cigar industry, but by the 1950s, as women everywhere were being elbowed out of the work force, the good jobs, rolling especially, were kept for men. The El Laguito factory was started by Celia Sanchez, the great guerilla commander and revered counterpart to Fidel Castro, as a place of employment for women. Although men were in management positions at El Laguito and we know that Fidel's cigars were rolled by a man, men were only hired as rollers at El Laguito three years ago. As early as 1961 the special cigars were made in a small workshop as a security measure conceived of in the Sierra Maestra. There was also a small factory in the Cabana fortress for rolling Che Guevara's cigars. Celia had the idea of selecting only women for this job, and Roberto Dimas Torres at Heroes del Moncada described it as a marriage of ideas since she was particularly interested in finding employment for "very modest women and children—widows and orphans of the war." Sanchez also trained women for employment in small factories producing chocolate and yogurt.

Sanchez started this factory in a splendid, eclectic-style villa set in a large garden. All the departments of a normal factory are present here, but they are somewhat eccentrically placed. A small garden house, perhaps once a guest house, located at the end of a long palm-lined path, holds the *tercios* of leaf tobacco. There is a cabin up another garden path where leaves are selected. Women sit in low chairs, smoothing the golden leaves. Women at El Laguito are dressed the same as at any other factory, with sun halters,

The factory where renowned Cohibas are produced occupies the villa called El Laguito, which provides workers with singularly elegant surroundings (*facing page*).

The entrance hall at El Laguito retains the tony atmosphere of the once-glamorous neighborhood after which the villa is named. For years the Cohiba factory produced Fidel Castro's personal cigars (*below*).

summer dresses, or cotton blouses with shorts or jeans. But here the atmosphere seems more carefree.

The factory buildings were renovated to celebrate Cohiba's 30th anniversary and outstanding financial success. Fresh paint might disturb the aroma of the cigars, but the owners realize that people want to see the corporate headquarters for one of the world's leading luxury items. The fact is, they cannot keep the house a secret for much longer. The walls of the villa and garden house, painted Wedgwood blue at least forty years ago, now show the effects of smoke, tropic dampness, and general wear and tear. The Venetian blinds are drawn and the colors are hardened by fluorescent lighting. In this atmosphere of dim light and dingy walls, these remarkably expensive and delicious Cohibas are rolled.

In the garden house the *tercios* are opened. The blender's office is nearby, at the end of the garden. He is tall, black, about forty years old, and completely forthright about his supply of golden leaves: he knows that they are gold, worth their featherlight weight on the world market. This little complex, seemingly unguarded and unmarked, is located about a block beyond the Palacio de Convenciones in the midst of embassies in one of the most well-protected areas of the city. The administration offices are located in a house at the other end of the property. In some ways it is the most architecturally distinguished of the buildings, with 1930s art deco glass and chrome, a spiral staircase, and oversized abstract floral designs in the detailing.

The new director is Emilia Tamayo Gonzalez, the first woman director of a Cuban tobacco factory, and she has worked at the factory for twenty of its thirty years. She is also the first person, apparently, to notice that this famous factory does not have an archive.

Previous pages: Celia Sanchez, Fidel Castro's revered counterpart, started the El Laguito factory to create jobs for "very modest women and children—widows and orphans of the war," though the factory's locale is anything but modest.

The Indian on the Cohiba label symbolizes a pristine time before the European discovery of tobacco.

The success of the brand has been phenomenal. They say it differs from all the other blends in three ways: the selection of leaves, the specific farms where they are grown, and an additional third fermentation of the leaves. This makes Cohiba milder than other brands in terms of taste and the fragrance of the smoke, though not in strength. In 1968 they produced three *vitolas*: lanceros, especiales, and panatelas. Robustos, esplendidos, and esquisitos were added to the roster next, and other shapes continue to be added. The head roller, Eduardo Rivero, is said to have produced the Cohiba blend specially for Fidel. The cigars seem to reflect modern taste: they do not have the strong smell, taste, or aroma characteristic of some of the older blends, but they do pack a wallop when smoked.

On the day of my visit to El Laguito, the color table contained eight "classes" of cigars. The head selector's window was closed and he used a fluorescent light to sort the colors: *encendido, colorado, colorado encendido, colorado pajijo* (my gift cigar, brown with red flecks), *verde, más verde, sangre de toro, verde botella.* These were all light cigars, though the *claros,* the lightest, were not on his table. He said that there are sixty-five or seventy colors. The sorted cigars are taken to the boxing table, where they are further sorted into groups of twenty-five closely related cigars. The cigars are boxed for one reason: to hide any defects. The twelve that have even the slightest irregularity get placed in the bottom layer. Any defect, such as a bumpy vein, a spot, a slight variation in color, is placed as much as possible away from view on the bottom layer of the box. Still, these twelve are arranged to look their best, left to right. That is why putting the ring on the cigar comes last, after cigar placement. The "mark," the jewel in the ring, is placed on the top of the best side of the cigar and the cigar is returned to the box. A sheet of cedar is inserted, and the top thirteen cigars, again presented with their best sides out, are placed in the box.

Almost imperceptibly, the lightest cigars go on the left and the dark on the right, with the ring added to advertise the brand and protect the cigar a little bit during the hour or two that it is smoked. The ring designates the best side of the cigar, which is what both the smoker and his associates see the most. The lid goes down. Everything after that consists of sealing the boxes and sending them into the world. Some brands put a stack of boxes in a press to even them out, to make them and their contents uniform for shipping and presentation. This is not necessary at Cohiba, because the cedar cigar box is strong, with thick sides and with little brass hinges and clasp. The boxes are wrapped in plain waxy paper. These boxes will protect the Cohiba as long as possible from the outside world and all the rough behavior of mankind.

Antonio Cornejo Cigar Box Factory
Established circa 1911
Avenida 20 de Mayo and Universidad, Centro Habana

This machine for producing cigar boxes was once used for four hours by Che Guevara. It is now reverently painted silver and retired from use.

Next to the Latinoamericano baseball stadium, there is a nondescript little factory with "1911" carved in the facade at Universidad Street. I have a friend who insists that he passes the building daily and never knew what went on inside. This is where the finely crafted cedar cigar boxes are made. Just inside the door is a machine, now painted with silver-aluminum paint and mounted on a base, which was once used for four hours by Che Guevara. Unlike cigar factories, it is filled with light, and the stacks of beautiful, light pink wood give off the cleanly pungent odor of a forest. Each box is assembled for the most part by hand, and the few machines—manufactured in Cleveland, Ohio—are polished from many years of use. Black market cigars are offered at cut-rate prices throughout the city, but the shoddy boxes of heavily shellacked plywood clearly show that they are counterfeit.

Although machines are used in the making of cigar boxes, a great deal of hand craftsmanship still goes into their production.

Overleaf: Unlike the cigar factories, the cigar box factory is filled with light and gives off the scent of cedar.

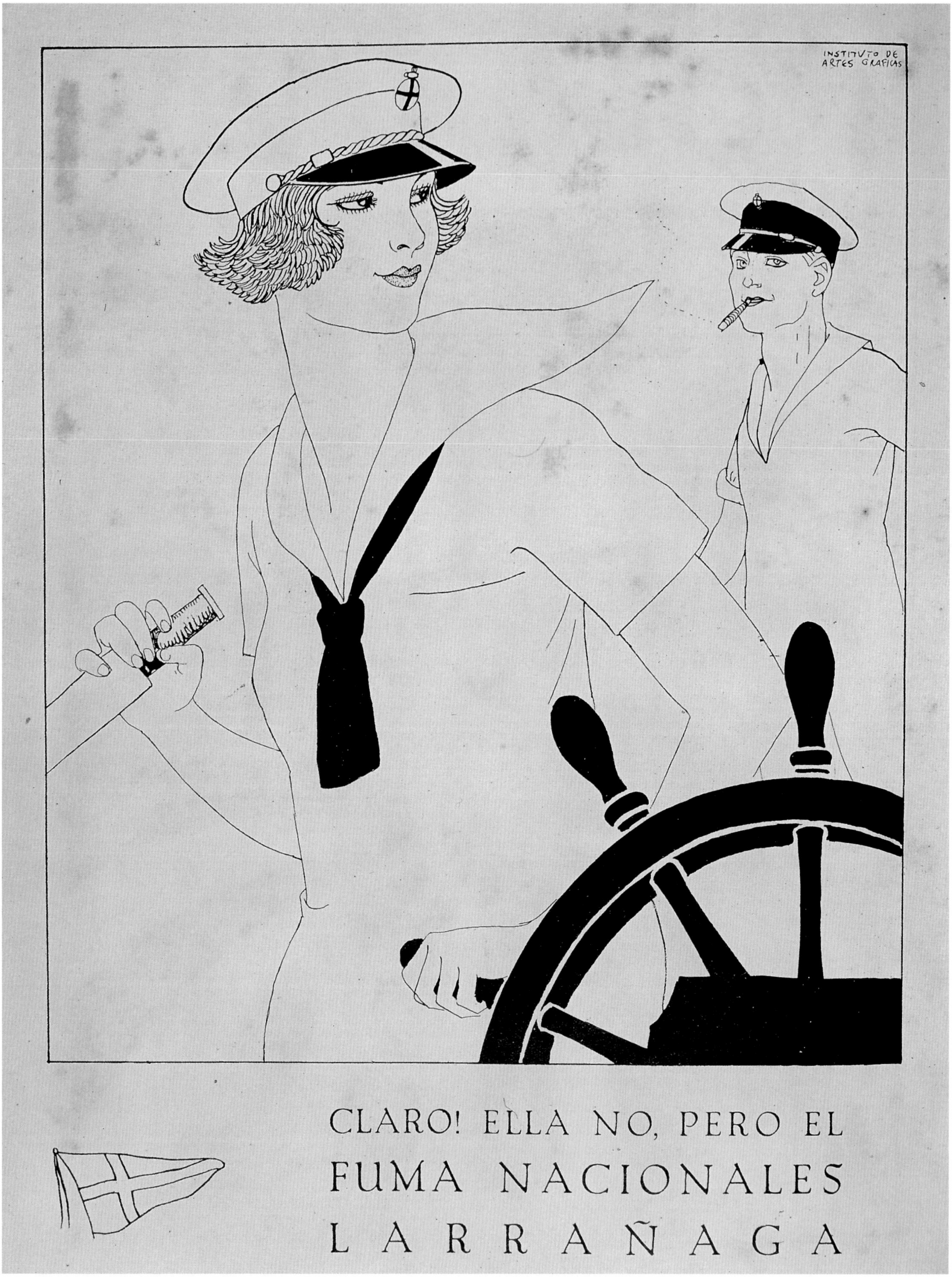

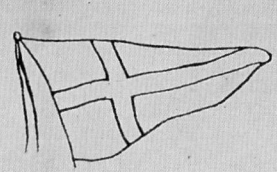

CLARO! ELLA NO, PERO EL
FUMA NACIONALES
LARRAÑAGA

FORMER EXPORT CIGAR FACTORIES

The former Por Larrañaga Factory
Established 1834 (to be reopened in 1998)
Currently known as Juan Cano Sainz
Carlos III (Salvador Allende) No. 713 (between Abiseca and Subirana)
Centro Habana

At Por Larrañaga all you can do is stand in the street and use your imagination. The lettering in cartouche at the top of the Por Larrañaga factory has been erased so the building seems anonymous. Two details stand out: the words "Established 1834" over the door, and a large plaque commemorating Carlos Rodriguez Careaga, a leader of tobacco workers who was assassinated in the city of Ciego de Avila on November 18, 1958 by Batista's troops. The plaque was signed in the memory of all the workers at Por Larrañaga.

The Por Larrañaga factory, renamed Juan Cano after the Revolution, is a handsome structure built around 1913. Its facade is lined with columns, but the graceful design has been ruined by a recent rooftop addition, which is fully visible from the street.

Por Larrañaga is one of the oldest Havana brands, established in 1834 by Antonio López and directed to prominence by Estaquio Alonso during the early years of this century. From 1910 to 1959 Por Larrañaga reigned as Havana's oldest established house in the cigar trade and received the greatest number of foreign visitors. One of the reasons Por Larrañaga was the cigar of style was because it was the brand chosen by Edward VII. Their national advertising campaign was orchestrated by Conrado Massaguer in his magazine *Social*. Here Massaguer taught the principles and traditions of cigar etiquette. Before the Revolution, when it was normal to smoke cigars in large quantities, what you smoked depended on the price of the cigar and your available cash. Por Larrañaga advertised its cigars in the context of style and social status, encouraging sports, nationalism, and club membership. After years of showing slender, debonair young men, Por Larrañaga ran a picture of a contented fat man who was, of course, smoking a Por Larrañaga. In Cuba, cigar etiquette requires allowing another man to light his cigar from your own; one of their advertisements depicted a very big, tough guy in cap and tweeds, looking like a boxer, leaning down to receive a light from the cigar of a very small, intimidated dandy. Two ashes touching, with the symbolic union of disparate social classes, seem to please the Cubans. I've seen cartoons of the man of the house and his servant praising the same brand.

Larrañaga also was instrumental in excluding women from cigar smoking and encouraging them to smoke cigarettes instead. They ran an advertisement in 1921 with a young woman standing at the helm of a yacht with the words, "Not for her." The male figure was smoking a Por Larrañaga.

Por Larrañaga advertisements often commented on contemporary social mores. This full-page ad (*facing page*) drawn by Conrado Massaguer and published in July 1921 in *Social* reads, "Not for her! But he smokes Larrañaga nacionales." Other advertisements published in *Social* include "With a good smoke even opposites meet" (top), October 1921, and "Control your nerves, not your pleasure" (bottom), November 1922. (Collection: Museum of the City of Havana)

131

The former José Gener Factory
Established 1867
Monte No. 51, Habana Viejo

The famous brands La Escepción, Hoya de Monterrey, Belinda, Gener, Punch, La Emperatriz de India, and Smart Set were all rolled at the José Gener factory. This is the only building of the five tobacco factories in the area that is no longer a cigar factory and is not even used for tobacco storage. It has been a printing plant for about twenty years.

The door is edged with *guardias entradas*, iron guards, which read "La Escepción" on one side and "José Gener" on the other. The building is four stories tall (the top floor was added at a later date) banded by iron balconies. On the ground floor, arcades cover the sidewalk along Monte Street and extend for an entire block along the side street, Agramonte. Lining the cornice are elaborate decorative white plaster crowns and the rest of the building is painted sea green. Glass doors etched with the initials "JHG" probably designate the entrance to the former cigar store.

The La Escepción brand was founded in 1867 by José Gener. On its label, the goddess of Industry holds the hand of Mercury. A Spanish crown with a small cross on top, in the middle of the label, is in the same style as the dozens of crowns that line the roof of the factory. There is an oval inset with gold medals. Cigar boxes labeled Hoyo de Monterrey and La Escepción are pictured at the lower edges. Although the factory itself is no longer in use, these blends are still produced, for the most part rolled at the La Corona factory.

The *guardias entradas*, or iron door guards, at the entrance of the former José Gener factory read JOSÉ GENER and LA ESCEPCIÓN, the brand that was founded by José Gener in 1867. The factory (*right*) has been a printing plant for about twenty years, and is the only one of the five tobacco factories in the area that is now neither a cigar factory nor used for tobacco storage.

The Calixto López factory, pictured in 1910 (*above and on the facing page*), was built in 1886 as part of a redevelopment plan. (Collection: Museum of the City of Havana)

Today the factory (*below*) is painted pink and functions as the national distribution center for cigars, cigarettes, and matches.

Calixto López
Established 1886
Agramonte No. 702, Habana Vieja

Two blocks away from the old José Gener factory, the Calixto López factory stands across the street from the train station and port. It was built in 1886 as part of the redevelopment plan, a three-story urban palace covering a city block. This cigar factory is currently the distribution center for cigars, cigarettes, and matches for domestic consumption. The facade is painted pink, and is dusty from the heavy traffic on the road along the port. When Calixto López was producing export cigars, Calixto López, Eden, Flor de López, Hermanos, Francisco C. Bances, Lo Mejor, Los Reyes de Espana, and Morro Castle were the house brands. The interior of the building is divided by temporary partitions, but the exterior is still beautiful.

The former Menéndez, García and Co.
Date unknown; now a warehouse
Virtudes No. 609, Centro Habana

The Menéndez, García and Co. factory, which looks more like a town house, is now used as a warehouse.

On Virtudes Street is a beautiful little two-story tobacco warehouse. In 1940 this was the factory where El Patio, H. Upmann, Montecristo, and Particulares were rolled.

The former Lobeto
Established 1930s
Monte No. 466, Centro Habana

The building seemed to be completely sealed, and it is hardly noticeable at first, but it is a handsome commercial building designed to look like, yes, a palace. The building is two stories with five bays of windows and arches facing this worn-out, heavily traveled old tobacco route. Decorative ironwork railings run the full length of the second story, forming a full balcony. I could imagine the cigar rollers standing in the windows, chatting in the fresh breeze and sunlight, as I'd seen several blocks away at the Partagás factory. There are large carved doors that must have made a handsome entrance. The building has recently been painted a bright lavender, but colors fade quickly in this sun, and soon the building will be covered with a layer of dirt and exhaust from buses, trucks, and cars that crowd the street.

The Lobeto factory, a handsome old building with beautiful carved doors and an iron balustrade, now stands empty.

Various Warehouses and a Union Hall

The city market on Monte Street is in a building that covers a block. As we were standing in front of the market, my friend told me that there were buildings nearby that he knew had been used for tobacco. I asked him to show them to me. We turned onto a small street, Manglar off Arroyo, and encountered a middle-aged man who confirmed that nearby there were two big buildings used for tobacco storage. On Lindero, Santa Maria, and Clavel streets are two large, well-kept buildings in an otherwise shoddy area. The streets were clean but deserted, and in the wind was the sharp scent, almost hot, of dried and cured tobacco. One building seemed to be sealed off. The other building had apartments on the top floor, but all the windows and doors were sealed on the ground floor. We followed the windowless walls of this building along Santa Maria, then turned onto Belascoain (also known as Padre Varela) to an eclectic building with vine and floral architectural decoration. At Belascoain 1058 a plastic sign reads "Procesadora de Hebra Rubia Segundo Quincosa"—*rubia* refers to the processing of a variety of red tobacco grown for cigarettes—named after a martyr of the Revolution. I was surprised that such a flamboyant, albeit somewhat down-at-heel, building had been consigned to tobacco. Later, I discovered that it had been a small tobacco warehouse owned by Constantine Gonzalez, an exporter; the warehouse had been pictured in an advertisement in *El Diario de la Marina* in 1932.

Three more large tobacco processing and storage houses in one small area were not on Perdomo's list in the 1940s. I began to realize that I had started out trying to find cigar factories and had instead discovered tobacco warehouses. We located two others about a block away on the other side of Padre Varela, across the street from the Academy of Music.

On Lealtad Street, from Carmen to Figueroas, a building that fills the entire block has "Syndicat Nacional de Tabacaleros SNT Tabacalera 1917–1945" carved in the facade. It seems like there are apartments above, or perhaps a day-care center, since there were women and children with toys on the central stairwell from the street. The tobacco business as well as a union hall occupy the ground floor. I concluded that there have always been unmarked tobacco storage houses in this area supplying the factories of El Rey del

The Constantino Gonzalez warehouse (*facing page*), for which this advertisement (*below*) appeared in 1932, is still used for tobacco storage. (Collection: Museum of the City of Havana)

The windowless wall of the former Constantino Gonzalez warehouse sharply contrasts its flamboyant facade.

Mundo, Romeo y Julieta, and Por Larrañaga five and ten blocks up Padre Varela Street, or Partagás and H. Upmann, located in a triangle to the north and east at the upper end of Monte Street.

Then it occurred to me that tobacco held here might be the famous supply of cured tobacco that is reserved for use only in the event of a crop failure. I never found out if this were true because Cubans wouldn't tell me. Cubans are sensitive and secretive about their cigar industry, and usually disclosed only the romance of the Vuelta Abajo and the romance of rolling a cigar. Another day, I visited Luaces Street in an area of Havana known as Little Hollywood. (Before the Revolution, European, Latin American, and U.S. film companies had offices in this area.) I wanted to photograph the mosaic-covered Centro Filmico building. At the edge of the little triangular park at Luaces and Bruzon is a building I'd passed before. Suddenly I noticed its sign: Cubatabaco Almacen de Tabaco. I asked the guard if they stored export tobacco there, and he nodded his head yes.

This colonnaded tobacco warehouse on Luaces Street is in "Little Hollywood," an area in Havana named for the European, Latin American, and American film companies that occupied the district before the Communist Revolution.

Overleaf: The hand colored seventeenth-century engraving of the entrance to Havana harbor belonging to Conrado Massaguer, the director of the magazine *Social,* was reproduced in that publication in June 1928. (Collection: Museum of the City of Havana)

Hombre de la Habana

THE HISTORY OF TOBACCO

Smoking rolled leaves of tobacco leaf is part of Cuban aboriginal culture and was first noted by Europeans in November 1492 on Christopher Columbus's first voyage to the West Indies. The Havana cigar as we know it—a cigar that is carefully twisted, rolled and wrapped with the finesse of a Saville Row tailor (as Cuban ethnographer Fernando Ortiz aptly put it), and exported throughout the world—is, however, a phenomenon of the eighteenth century.

Since tobacco was first seen by Europeans when they discovered the island, studying its history is like studying the history of the country. It is a history of colonialism, repression, and trade shenanigans. The history of cigars, in that context, is like a liberation movement with many skirmishes. It is still in progress.

The story conveniently begins with Columbus. Ortiz has carefully analyzed the diary entries and shipping records, and it appears that from Columbus's point of view, tobacco leaves, rolled up, were just another splendid curiosity from the Americas. Tobacco was, if anything, a novelty to be taken back to his Spanish Catholic sponsors, Ferdinand and Isabella, something to be planted in European gardens. Columbus's voyages were commercial ventures with well-documented plans for turning a profit. He introduced certain items to Cuba in the overall scheme to make colonization produce income, such as cattle and sugar cane, which would eventually become a popular cash crop. Any money that could be derived immediately from his "discoveries" would have been noted in his journals and other voluminous literature that surrounded the conquest of the Americas. Because tobacco was unknown in Europe, there was no demand for it, and we can be sure that it was not considered to be a "product" in Columbus's time.

This engraving entitled "Man of Havana" (*facing page*), dating from 1800 and reproduced in *Social* in February 1929, demonstrates the importance of the cigar to Cuban social identity. (Collection: Museum of the City of Havana)

Tobacco appears in the journals as powdered tobacco, or *cohoba*, which was used by the Indians in ceremony. Columbus wrote admiringly of the polished wooden bowl that held the pulverized, dried tobacco leaves, and of a little forked pipe used to inhale tobacco through the nostrils. His voice in these entries is that of an entrepreneur or businessman when it isn't that of an anthropologist. He carried tobacco items back to Spain on his ships, but there is no written record of this cargo. It seems that tobacco was a mere curiosity among Europeans at first.

One of the interesting things about the Spanish conquest of the Americas is the number of observers present. Other writers such as Bartolomeo de Las Casas, Father Pane, López de Gomara, and Captain Gonzalo Fernandez de Oviedo discussed the ceremonial aspects and the use of tobacco at length, some with interest and respect and some with prejudice. For example, Oviedo's text, published in 1535, calls using tobacco a vice that makes those who indulge lose their senses. On the other hand, it was administered to the sick. Everyone agreed on one point, however: it altered one's state of mind.

The Europeans' initial reaction to tobacco set the style for the future. It was both coveted and forbidden, but it took some time for the European population to learn about the chronicles of Oviedo and Las Casas and decide for themselves whether it was savage or stylish.

Cubans like to say that they were discovered three times: first by Christopher Columbus, then by Alexander von Humboldt, and finally by their own Fernando Ortiz. In his book *Cuban Counterpoint: Tobacco and Sugar*, Ortiz looks at the relationships between the sailors and the port, the port and taverns, taverns and women, and in doing so adds a great deal to the tapestry of tobacco history.

Sailors were the first great exporters of tobacco and the earliest Europeans to determine how it was used. Starting in 1492 and for the next three hundred years, Cuban tobacco left the shores as plug tobacco to chew; snuff, or pulverized tobacco to sniff; and twist, a coil of rolled tobacco to smoke in a pipe. It was a pair of Columbus's sailors who reported the first instance of smoking rolled leaves. They are thought to be the first European smokers.

When the rich decided they too wanted to use tobacco, they adopted the sailor's choices, primarily pipes and snuff. When tobacco was finally appropriated by the rich and stylish, they had a lot of fun with it, handcrafting pipes, commissioning elaborate snuff boxes, attending smoking schools, and forming smoking clubs. The story of the cigar always gets lost at this point in history. Gentlemen's albums, our other documents regarding tobacco, are filled with pipes, pipe smokers, pouches, and snuff boxes—but no cigars. By the end of the sixteenth century in England and France tobacco became popular and stylish even though it always carried with it the rationale that it was also a medicine. Certainly tobacco was used as a mild painkiller and offered some relief. The back pages of tobacco albums are filled with treatises on tobacco as medicine. The cigar gets squeezed out, reduced to an aromatic puff of smoke in the annals of history. In reality, although tobacco

Construction began on the Castillo de los Tres Reyes del Morro, better known as El Morro Castle, in 1589. This fort, together with the Real Fuerza and La Punta, protected Havana's harbor and lucrative shipping trade from pirates (*facing page*).

manufactured into snuff, plug, and twist was coming into Europe, it is believed that nobody quite knew how to roll cigars, so cigars were not introduced to the rest of the world until much later.

During the early 1500s in Havana, where Spanish fleets assembled before they set out across the ocean in convoy, tobacco was a trade commodity. Columbus, however, did not consider it an article of trade, nor did his son Diego, nor, it appears, did anyone else who was dealing in official commerce at the time. Eventually the Spanish realized that there was a sub-rosa trade in tobacco among the sailors. The Spanish officials who colonized Cuba spent the next three centuries trying to regain control of the trade. They were never satisfied with a percentage of the profit; they wanted all of it. Since the plant could be grown anywhere on the island and nearly every inch of coastline was open to pirates, the tobacco trade was almost uncontrollable. The Spanish attempt to gain control over tobacco came too late because an entire system for procurement, shipping, and marketing was already in place. Those who opposed Spain and joined the underground trade in tobacco included, aside from England and France, peoples of Cuba, Mexico, and the surrounding islands of the Caribbean, and a significant number of slaves.

Each year sailors waited in Havana, often for months at a time, for the Spanish fleet to assemble. Ships came from Cartagena, Nombre de Dios, Portobello, Vera Cruz, Campeche, and Santo Domingo—everywhere in the Americas, or New Spain as it was then called—and stopped at the Havana customs house to inventory goods.

Havana's harbor is naturally shaped to provide protection from pirates and hurricanes with a small entrance at the mouth of the harbor and a huge bay where ships gathered. Between 1519 and 1590 several towers and three major fortresses were constructed around the bay. The Castillo de La Real Fuerza is a fortified and moated castle located just inside the bay. Construction began in 1558, after the pirate Jacques de Sores burned Havana in 1555. The new city grew around this fort. In 1589 construction began on the fortified Castillo de San Salvador de la Punta (La Punta) and on a fort directly across the harbor, the Castillo de los Tres Reyes del Morro (Morro Castle). Both of these are enormous fortresses.

Pirates knew better than to try to enter Havana. In an immensely popular book of the time called *Buccaneers of America*, the notorious Henry Morgan described Havana as "one of the renowndst and strongest places of all the West Indies."

The ships were unloaded and the contents stored in the customs house along with the fantastic gold and silver booty from the Americas. Finally, the ships were reloaded and the fleet set out in convoy, protected by the armadas, on their run from Havana to Spain. Thousands of people anticipated the fleet's departure, and in port everyone needed food, drink, and diversions. Taverns opened up all over Havana to cater to the waiting sailors. Presumably Spanish officers and traders stayed with people who had houses, but the huge transient population depended on the taverns. The owners and managers of

This line drawing of a woman smoking a cigar, from an album dated 1835, reflects the era's changing attitudes toward women and smoking (*facing page*). (Arents Collection, New York Public Library)

Overleaf: In a watercolor of a fashionable Picadilly salon from an album dating from 1836, cigar smoking has a prominent role. (Arents Collection, New York Public Library)

149

Piccadilly Saloon

the taverns were mostly black women, according to Fernando Ortiz. (The Spanish brought black slaves with them to Cuba, and imported Africans to build the forts and later to develop the sugar cane fields.) Some black female slaves in Havana of the 1520s, '30s, and '40s were able to purchase their freedom. These "tripe-selling Negresses" also sold tobacco in their taverns. Since nobody really knew how to use tobacco, there must have been a great deal of experimentation. Chewing, sniffing, and smoking, along with the usual eating, drinking, and gossiping, must have been the activities of the day. These businesses served the town, in essence maintained the fleet, and sold plenty of tobacco for immediate consumption, for the voyage, and for future sale in Seville. Indians were suppliers, farmers, and leaf curers. Besides the taverns, there were opportunities to sell tobacco outside Havana in the many small islands off the coast where pirates harbored.

In the 1550s the Spanish finally caught on to the fact that people other than themselves were making profits from the sale of tobacco. Up until that time it was not illegal to publicly sell these leaves. The first restriction against the sale of tobacco, in the year 1557, coincided with a city ordinance specifically aimed at the businesses that were run by black women. They were forbidden to have taverns or inns, or to sell wine or tobacco, under penalty of fifty lashes. It was an exceptionally harsh statute specifically directed against black women. Later, the restrictions were extended to everyone, with the penalties doubled if the transgressors were African.

It is clear that trading in tobacco was not stopped; another group simply grabbed the profit. From the mid-sixteenth century onward, the privilege of tobacco trade fell to the Spanish in Cuba, or, as Ortiz puts it, "Tobacco worked its way up." The white man had taken over the domain of the Indians and blacks.

The beginning of the sixteenth century is the start of the first commercial monopoly. All revenues from the Americas went to Spain. Yet the Spanish were so inept at handling this particular commodity that their failure to manage tobacco was a precursor of what was to come: the Spanish would ultimately lose complete control of the commodity. If dried tobacco could be smuggled out, so could seeds.

Soon, people around the world were growing it. Tobacco was being grown in China in 1573, brought by Spaniards from the Philippines; in India, Indo-China, and Java by 1600, taken by Portuguese traders and missionaries; in Japan in 1605, also via Portuguese traders; and it had spread throughout the Mediterranean, via Spanish sailors, reaching Turkey by 1605.

Tobacco cultivation quickly spread during the seventeenth century. John Rolfe, the husband of Pocahontas, secured a crop for Virginia in 1612 and the competition was on. In Virginia it was cultivated on a large scale using a large number of slaves. By contrast, in Cuba the cultivation of tobacco had always been done on a garden scale. Even the largest tobacco growers had only two or three slaves who worked in the cultivation.

Tobacco was an irresistible contraband garden crop which could be grown anywhere by anyone and smuggled to market. Again the Spanish went to extreme lengths to gain control: in Cuba in 1606 cultivation was forbidden entirely. In 1614 the ban was lifted, but the entire crop had to be sent to Seville. Disobedience was punishable by death. Yet Cuban tobacco continued to be grown, and then sold in London. While Virginia tobacco was readily available, Cuban was the connoisseur's choice. Cuban tobacco sold outside Spain was a contraband commodity for about a century, but in reality sailors had never stopped buying tobacco. This was the period of English and French piracy against the Spanish, and tobacco, because of its rareness, was one of the preferred items. At the end of the sixteenth century, although tobacco was in Europe, it was not there in any significant quantity; a hundred years later it was one of the most widely cultivated plants on the planet.

In England, Sir Walter Raleigh made tobacco a popular accoutrement of court life. Finding Raleigh smoking one day, a servant threw water on him. Whether this is fact or folktale, many engravings illustrated the story. The court of Elizabeth I adored smoking; they perfected blowing smoke rings which they called "wonderful configurations." The Elizabethans especially seemed to have a great deal of fun smoking and dreaming about places that produced the exotic plant. In a play called *Lady Alimony,* a character is called a "Mundungo Monopolist" for the black tobacco in which he traded. He is also called a "Cashiered Consort" who had "smook'd himself into a Mercenary title of Knightship."

By the seventeenth century the use of tobacco was firmly established in Europe. Tobacco historian W. F. Fairholt, writing in 1859, depicts many examples of seventeeth-century pipes, tobacco pouches, and instruments to tamp down pipe tobacco. All were highly ornamental. Exquisitely designed snuff boxes, were admired by the French, and were, in fact, made throughout Europe and Asia. The Dutch painted pipe smokers.

In the eighteenth century the throne of Spain was administered by the Bourbon kings who initiated reforms and streamlined the mercantile system to extract more revenue from the Americas. Certain merchants were licensed to export commodities, with a portion of the return going to the king. In 1717 the crown declared tobacco a royal monopoly. In 1740 the Royal Company of Havana was founded to oversee procurement from the Cuban growers and to collect duty taxes, with its ultimate goal being to supply Cuban tobacco to the Royal Factories of Seville. Martín de Arostegui, who held the first tobacco contract in 1739, was founder and president of the Royal Company. The monopoly fixed prices, essentially driving out the established growers and discouraging new investment in tobacco farming. The tobacco farmers resisted selling their crops to the monopoly. Only small-scale farmers could take the risk of going into the business of producing the plant and eventually tobacco growing was the small farmer's domain, with whites and free blacks raising tobacco on plots that averaged only thirty-three acres.

Overleaf: Martín de Arostegui, whose house is pictured here, held the first tobacco contract in Cuba in 1739 and was the founder of the Royal Company tobacco monopoly.

THE MODERN HAVANA CIGAR

Firing cannonballs through the walls of the Morro Castle, the English captured and occupied Havana in 1762; then after ten months they traded Havana back to the Spanish in exchange for the Floridas. The break in the Spanish tobacco monopoly can be traced to 1763, when "Havana" cigars traveled to England and America. To paraphrase Fernando Ortiz, they traveled in the pockets of the red coats of the British officials returning to England, and to Boston and Baltimore in the blue coats of the Yankee officers in charge of the colonial American regiments that assisted in the Havana occupation. During the brief occupation, Spanish officials were sent home to Spain. Civil servants, Spanish priests, and soldiers, as Ortiz put it, "clung to the expensive and aristocratic vice of smoking Havana cigars, which they had sent them from Cuba."

The Florida holdings (now lower portions of Alabama, Mississippi, all of Florida, and parts of Louisiana) were a tremendous territorial loss for Spain. On one hand, Spain was able to reclaim Havana in 1764, and the royal monopoly could resume its exclusive hold on tobacco. On the other hand, after those ten months under the British, the Spanish lost their iron grip on the port of Havana. In the following years of the century, port entries increased from just six ships per year, recorded just prior to the capture, to two hundred. Within a decade thousands of ships had sailed in and out of the port. For the first time, Havana cigars—made of Cuban tobacco and rolled in the special way of the Cubans—were smoked throughout the world.

According to Oscar Zanetti, director of Cuba's Institute of History, Cuban tobacco growers and the Canary Islands, which lay off the coast of Africa and belong to Spain, have a long history of association. Nearly all the farmers in Cuba were from the Canary Islands. Spain was always attempting to colonize New Spain, and Canary Islanders were invited to participate in one immigration scheme offering relocation to Pensacola, in the Floridas, with a stopover in Havana for provisions. The success of this venture was doubtful since there was no commercial economy in Florida, so many Canarians simply stayed in Havana or left the Florida settlement and returned to Cuba. In 1763, when Havana was returned to Spain, the Spanish made no provisions for transporting the settlers from the former colonies back to Spain. At the outset of the English occupation of Florida, most Spanish families had no desire to live under English rule. Unable to return to Spain, they made their way to nearby Cuba. The country was nearly empty outside Havana, but favorable terms for populating the interior were offered. Tobacco was a crop that a skillful farmer from the Canaries could produce.

Cuba's elite was composed of a few Spaniards at the top followed by Cubans of European decent. The latter consisted of small farmers around Havana who raised tobacco or foodstuffs, workers for the tobacco monopoly, and finally, since Cuba was covered in pine forests, workers in the shipbuilding industry. This emerging society had been born in Cuba and had a stake in the economy.

Martín de Arostegui, the president of the tobacco monopoly, on the other hand, was a Spaniard born in Navarre. His brother, Martín Esteban (the custom of naming both sons by the same name in case one dies is characteristic of the eighteenth century) held the rank of brigadier general in the army and commanded the local cavalry regiment of Havana. Both men held powerful political appointments. Arostegui, licensed by the crown to control tobacco, was assured of a fortune. He built a large house in 1759 that still exists at Tacon No. 4 just outside the walls of the Castillo de La Real Fuerza. From the second-story gallery Arostegui would have been able to see the ships being loaded for Spain, and their departure past the Morro Castle and into the outside channel. It was his job to ship the tobacco quota established by the crown.

Historian Maria de Carmen Morales García has assembled shipping reports from the eighteenth century which show that more pounds of tobacco were being shipped than were being reported. In 1746 the quota of tobacco to be sent is 33,913 pounds, but 36,829 pounds were shipped to the Canaries before being transported to Seville. In 1754 the quota was 136,202 pounds and shipping records show 218,950 pounds arrived in the Canary Islands. Those discrepancies indicate that 72,748 pounds of tobacco never reached Seville and apparantly went from the Canaries to France, Germany, and England.

The monopoly was famous throughout the world for its mismanagement. A 1770 book on tobacco, *Verhandeling van den Tabak*, complains about the administration in Seville: "The tobacco of Havana annually brings the king of Spain 2,427,803 crowns. The income is drawn from one large sale when the king allows this merchandise to be sold for the account of the royal treasury. The management of this is entrusted to one of his majesty's administrators. If necessary measures were taken in the sale of this tobacco, which is very popular in Spain and other states, especially that prepared in Seville, this income could be increased to five or six million. The indifference of the Spanish alone is to blame for the small quantity of tobacco which they export."

By the turn of the century the crown had agreed to acknowledge what the world already knew, and commissioned an official report regarding the abuses of the Havana monopoly. They then slowly went about abolishing it. During its hundred years of existence, tobacco farmers had engaged in open conflict with the monopoly. One incident stands out. In 1716 the growers mutinied against an inspector who came to fix the price for their crops. They repeated their rebellion in 1721 and 1723. That year, five hundred farmers refused to accept the terms and destroyed the fields of those who did accept. A cavalry sent to quell the rebellion killed several of the farmers and strung them up in trees on the hilltop of Jesus del Monte overlooking Havana. In the Pinar del Rio public library there is a book illustrating this lynching. A wood engraving depicts men hanging from trees with soldiers wearing metal armor and helmets and holding long-handled hatchets as weapons. The site of the lynching is the pilgrimage church built in 1698, now the reconstructed church Jesus del Monte, on the highest hill overlooking all of Havana. Cuban tobacco historian Rivero Muñiz says the farmers were shot near Santiago de las Vegas (a famous old town in Havana province named for its tobacco fields) and their bodies were carried to the hill, where they were hung as a warning to the rebels. Tobacco farmers became symbols of men resisting oppression. They had a legitimate gripe, wanting to be able to trade in their much-coveted crop and get a fair price for it. And it appeared that the country sympathized with them.

Ortiz writes that in Europe during the Napoleonic Wars, Spain was crossed and recrossed by troops from all over Europe who learned to smoke cigarettes and cigars, creating a market demand that Spain could not meet. Previously these lovely little tubes of tobacco had been exclusive gifts, *regalias*, of the court of Spain. Suddenly they were in demand everywhere.

The Spanish eventually realized that a more laissez-faire attitude would stimulate the economy. In 1825 all restrictions were abolished and trade in Havana cigars, especially sales to the United States and Europe, made them available to everyone around the world. Jean Stubbs, English historian of Cuban tobacco, writes that exports increased rapidly from 140 million cigars in 1840 to nearly 360 million cigars in 1855, the peak year, when new markets in Germany, Denmark, and France were added to the existing markets of England, the United States, and Spain.

This wood engraving, which reads "Ballad of the Tobacco Farmers' Uprising," illustrates the lynching of tobacco growers who rebelled in 1716 against official price fixing of their crops. The engraving is from *Tabaco Poema* by Andres de Piedra-Bueno, published in Havana in 1944.

ROMANCE DE LA
SUBLEVACION DE
LOS VEGUEROS

CAUSE AND EFFECT.
YOUNG HOPEFUL.—Suffocate the children?—What nonsense you talk, mother! Do 'em good!—kill the insects.

The popularity of the modern export cigar soared during the nineteenth century, as indicated by these satirical engravings. (Arents Collection, New York Public Library)

This wagon barn, built by the Susini Cigar and Cigarette Factory, is located across the street from the terminus of Cuba's first railroad, which came from the old tobacco producing city of Bejucal.

LA CABANA
MADE FOR
THE GREAT EXHIBITION
1851
PRESENTED BY
ROBERT LEWIS
19 ST JAMES'S STREET LONDON

La Cabana sent these cigars (*facing page*),
which received a first-place medal, to the
Great Exhibition of 1851 in London. (Tabacco
Museum, Havana.) Nineteenth-century wood
engraving (*below*). (Arents Collection, New
York Public Library.)

EARLY EXPORT CIGARS

In Cuba, cigars are referred to as *tabacos,* the same word used for the plant.
However, in Spain they were called *cigarros,* and the name stuck throughout
the rest of the world. A *cigarro* is a cicada found in Andalusia, and the earliest
cigars in Spain were said to resemble these insects in shape,
size, and color. That describes, fairly clearly, what early cigars
looked like. They had broad bodies, were dark in color, and
measured perhaps three and a half inches in length and probably three-quarters of an inch wide, pointed on each end. In
Spain there was an attempt to give them another name, *tubano,*
but it never replaced *cigarro.* Although Cubans allowed their
tabacos to be marketed abroad under the Spanish popular name,
they have never accepted it themselves. Cubans did use the
Spanish word *regalias* to name the cigars they exported first.
They created new shapes and gave them names that were often
descriptive. The concha resembled spiralled mollusks. A row of
dried figs, usually strung together, became a spongy brown
tube, and are the image for brevas. The panatela could be
named after a small sea sponge of that name that has a smooth

outer surface, is tube-shaped, and has an inner webbing that spirals from the
center.

There were also *regalias chicas* and *medias,* small and medium sized.
The first uncontrolled export market for Havana cigars was London. In addition to conchas and brevas, the Cabañas y Carvajal factory sent regalias,

A cigar shop on the masthead of Paul Pry's *The Penny and Spirit of the Town* (*right*). (Arents Collection, New York Public Library.) Nineteenth-century wood engraving (*below*). (Arents Collection, New York Public Library.)

embajadores, regalias imperiales, regalia de la reina ("a gift for the queen"), londres, and operas (for smoking at the opera).

Cabañas had been rolling cigars of all sizes and shapes and marketing them in Europe and the United States for about half a century before it was awarded a gold medal for first place in the Great Exhibition of 1851 in London. A few of these cigars still exist, carefully preserved under glass. By 1859, a merger had apparently taken place and the factory was called H. De Cabañas y Carvajal, located at 92 San Ignacio Street, and owned by Anselmo Gonzales del Valle. They had a line of ten cigars listed by size—to some degree this means importance—with the largest first: Napoleones, Escepcionales, Embajadores, Regalias, Imperiales, Regalia de la Reina, Regalia chica, Media regalia de Londres, Cazadores, Cilindrados, Londres, Brevas or Prensados, Damas or Entreactos, Medianos or Galanes, Tabaquitos cigarros (cigarettes), and Caballeros or Panatelas.

Havana cigars have always been luxury items throughout the world. Ortiz states this clearly: "It was never considered common to smoke Havana cigars, even in Spain. They were always expensive, and Spain was poor for centuries, even under the pomp and circumstance of the Habsburgs."

If you look at the early shipping advertisements for cigars, they seem to have been sold according to their shapes, as well as their brand names. Cigars exported to the United States have brand names such as Washington, Empire City, and Knickerbocker, as well as *vitolas* (designations based on shape and size) like conchas, regalias, and brevas. Advertisements placed by importers in New Orleans read like lists of these brand names and *vitolas*. What is surprising is the volume of cigars on the New Orleans market. For instance, during one week in January 1859, Bornio & Bros., at 34 Gravier

Street in New Orleans, placed an advertisement for 1,600,000 fine Havana cigars. He was not alone. S. De Visser & Co., at 74 Magazine Street, offered 530,000, and P. Guma, located on the corner of Canal and Tchoupitoulas advertised "Cigars, landing ex brigs M.A. Stevens and Tullulah from Havana, 375,000 cigars."

Ortiz explains that import taxes were one reason for these large shipments. "For instance, in 1856 there were a number of cigar workers idle in Havana, owing to the fact that in 1855, in addition to a large amount of leaf tobacco, 356,582,500 cigars were exported, the greatest volume of export trade Cuba had ever known. This happened because the United States market wanted to stock up before the sharp increase in customs duties effective March 3, 1857."

THE STORY OF LABELS

There are scrapbooks filled with Havana cigar labels at the Museum of the City of Havana. Starting with the earliest labels, it is possible to trace the story of the Havana cigar through pictures.

Beginning in about 1825, Cubans were finally able to sell tobacco without restrictions, liberated at last from the Spanish tobacco monopoly. For three centuries tobacco had been called a pleasurable plant or an evil weed, a devilish desire or a luscious pastime, depending on who was telling the story. Cubans understood that their product was both good and evil, but for the first time they would be allowed to tell their story, and they had to decide how they wanted to market their product. One method was the cigar label.

Labels, often quite small, were printed or stamped on paper and attached to bales or barrels of export tobacco. One example, pipe and chewing tobacco from the factory of Juan De Dios, located at 43 San Juan Street in Puerto

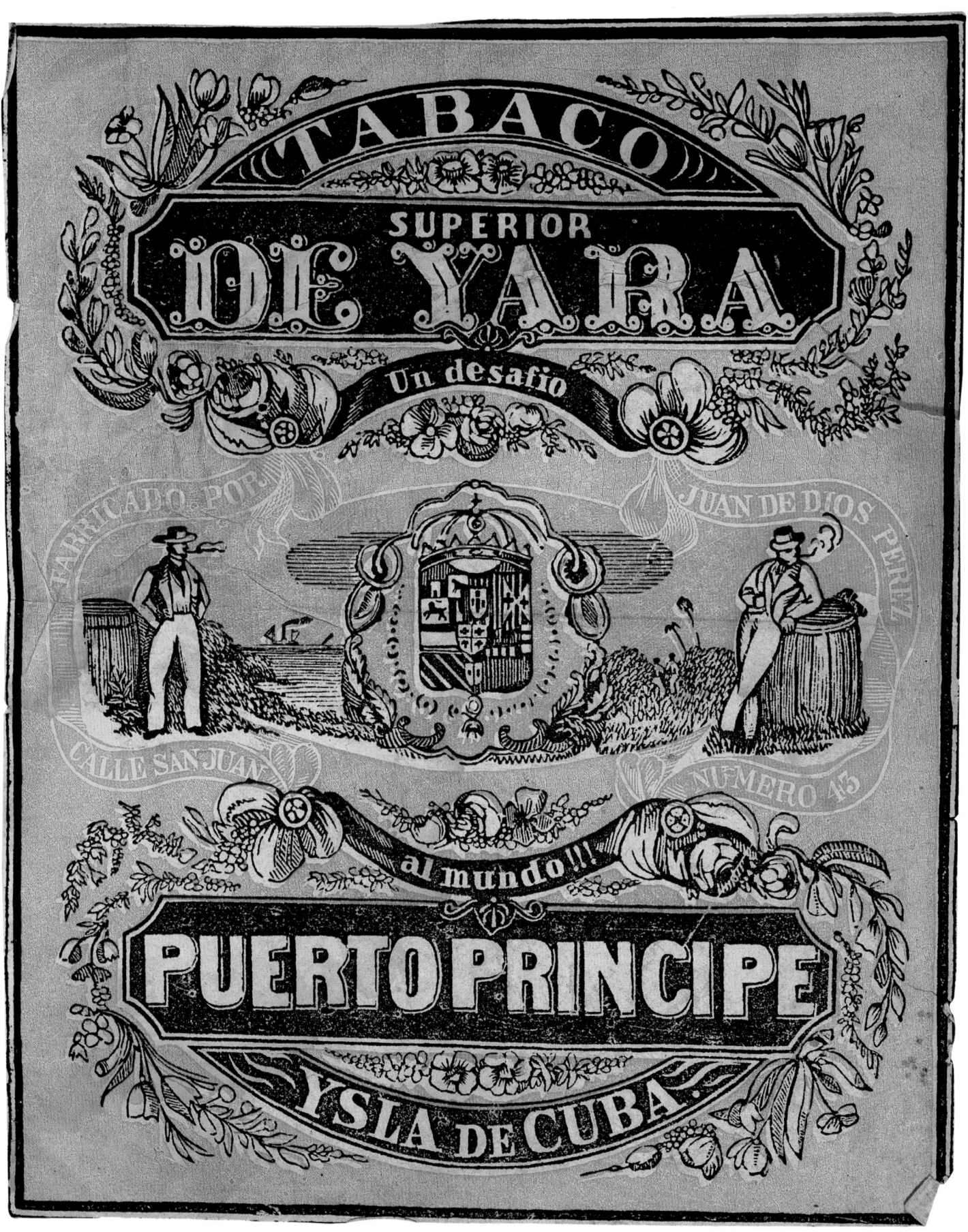

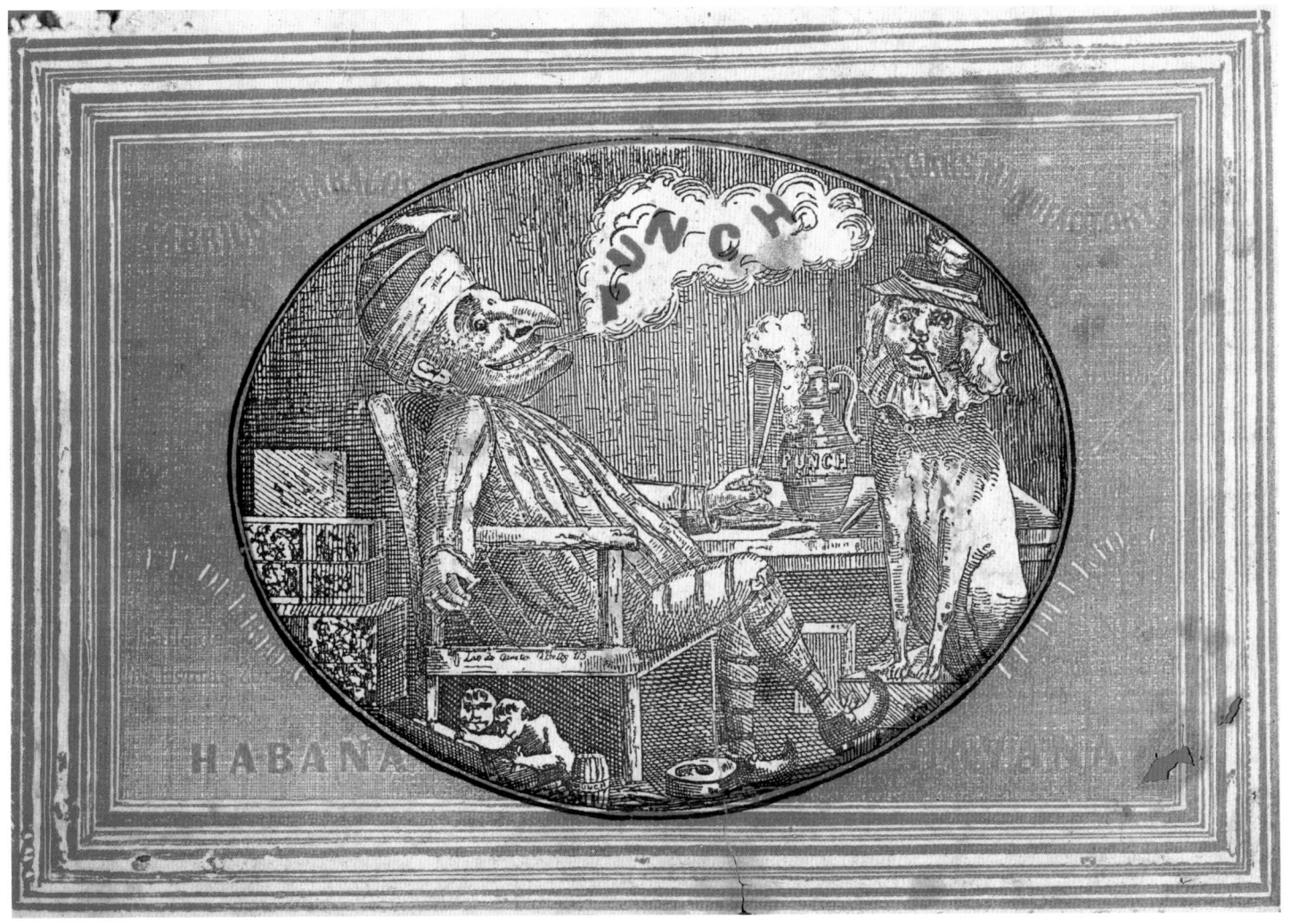

Principe, advertised the famous Yara tobacco with pictures of sailors, wearing waxed canvas pants, smoking and leaning on shipping barrels. Cigar labels always carried the name and address of the owner. Sometimes a small illustration was added, which could be a simple frame of roses around the words, or a ship or a star. Labels were used long before the cigar box was developed, but once inside the box, they became much more elaborate decorations telling the story of the Havana cigar.

Cuban cigar labels extolled the tobacco plant, usually picturing one or two in flower. If the country's reputation can be summed up in one image, it is the tobacco plant left to flower and produce seeds. The flower is small and delicate on the husky plant; its blossom is pink, and Cubans like to point out that it is in the shape of a five-pointed star, another symbol of Cuba. This single tobacco plant in flower is always used as an icon, often shown curved like the laurel leaf into a wreath, or in front of bales of tobacco leaf or shipments of cigars on the Havana dockside.

The most enduring image of all is the small tobacco field, called a *vega*, surrounding a farmer's modest house. The early tobacco farmers were Spaniards, many from the Canary Islands, who lived in one-story adobe houses similar to the one featured on the Cubrey and Valero label. The

Label, c. 1840, for Tabaco de Yara, manufactured by Juan de Dios Pérez, Calle San Juan No. 45, Puerto Principe, Cuba (*facing page*). (Arents Collection, New York Public Library)

Label, c. 1859, for Punch cigars, manufactured by F. P. Del Río y Ca., Figuras Street No. 20, Havana (*above*). (Arents Collection, New York Public Library)

tobacco farmers on the labels, and also in reality, live in small, square houses called *bohios*, thatched with palm fronds. This architecture was originally used by the Taino Indians of Cuba and is not a Spanish style. The simple house and field on the label presents a sympathic scene and is a far cry from the vast estates of the Spanish oligarchy.

On labels, tobacco farmers in white shirts and trousers, with wide-brimmed, low-crowned straw hats banded with black ribbon, plow their fields with oxen or cultivate the soil by hand. Or they simply stand smoking a cigar, as in the Inmejorables label, on which El Montero stands by his horse, with faithful dogs at his feet. *Monteros* were cattlemen who worked on the big haciendas around Havana. They were Creoles, mulattos, and slaves. Here, perhaps, is the world's first Marlboro man. He wears a machete on his belt, a symbol of labor as well as independence. The roof of his small house is in the background; a faithful wife most likely is inside. Morning glories, sweet peas, and passion flowers—the flowers of the countryside—frame the picture. A single tobacco plant in flower is located near the dogs. Out of the man's mouth curves the phrase: *"No reconozco rival"* ("No recognizable rival"), praising the cigar and himself. In 1825, no one could match the tobacco farmer in contentment and independence. In the eighteenth century he had been viewed as a single man against the tobacco monopoly, a kind of pastoral revolutionary. Now he has attained his dreams.

Originally *vegas* were tobacco fields, usually bottomlands along a river, but later the word came to mean entire regions where tobacco is produced. On the early labels that picture tobacco fields, a stream runs along one edge of the field, and there is usually a mountain in the background, as in the Cubrey y Valero label. The mountain provides shade and protection for the tobacco, and is the source of the stream. *Vuelta abajo* means "the slope below," and refers to the western end of Cuba, topographically lower than Havana. This famous area, a plateau with sweeping mountains to block the strong afternoon sun, is the finest agricultural area for tobacco in Cuba. Sometimes the picture on the label includes a rising sun, sharp-edged with multicolored rays, indicating a new day for Cuban tobacco.

The beautiful royal palm, tall and as straight as an arrow, is Cuba's national tree. Although it decorates the landscape, it also has a utilitarian function in the Cuban tobacco industry, often providing the building material for tobacco barns. (Tobacco barns, which are called houses in the tobacco lexicon, are shaped like an inverted V, with a roof covered entirely in palm fronds.) In addition, the tree sheds a layer of its trunk annually, providing an ideal organic packaging material for shipping tobacco. This method has been used for centuries because the bark breathes, retains moisture, and has an elasticity that protects the bundles of leaves inside. The bark-wrapped *tercio* bale is used as a symbol of export tobacco, and is often shown sitting on the Havana dockside, sometimes with a female goddess such as Commerce comfortably seated on it, waiting for the next ship out. Today collecting palm bark has become a major secondary industry.

The label for El Montero cigars, manufactured by Inmejorables, San Lazaro No. 196, Havana, advises that there is "no recognizable rival" (*facing page*). (Arents Collection, New York Public Library)

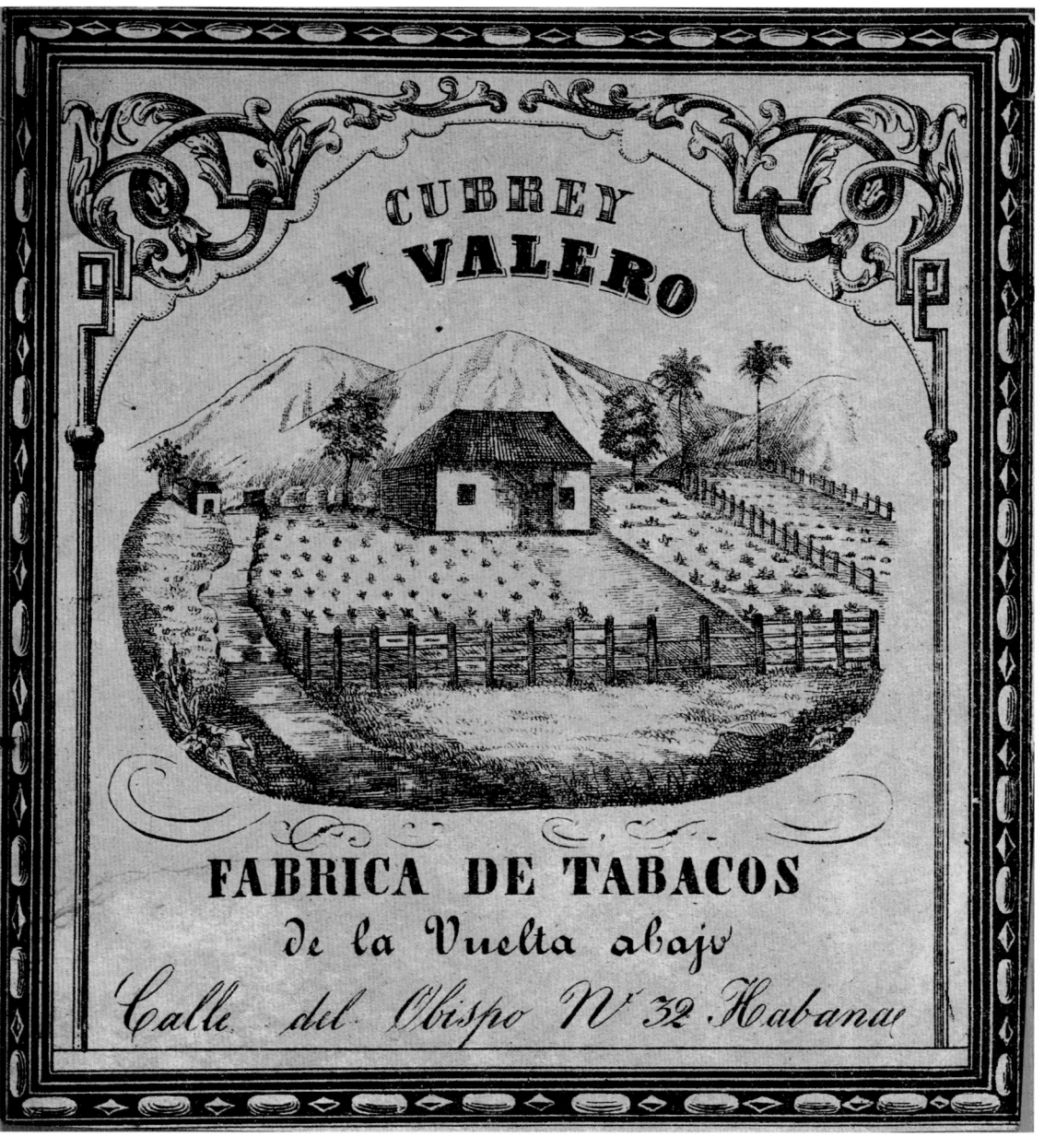

The 1840 label for Cubrey y Valero cigars, Obispo Street No. 32, Havana, shows the perfect *vega*: small fields, the farmer's house, royal palms, and a stream descending from the mountains. (Arents Collection, New York Public Library)

Some of the oldest labels have plantains or banana plants growing near the farmer's house. The leaves were used in nursery gardens, according to the *Cartilla Rústica*. The tobacco seeds were planted in the middle of forests, and the big green plantain leaves were used to cover the tiny seeds. Now fine nylon netting is used to cover the seeds, but as recently as thirty years ago plantain leaves were being used to protect the seedbeds.

Legalidad, the factory of Sanchez López, used a picture of a three-masted ship in full sail leaving the Havana harbor, framed by cornucopias of flowers, to represent export cigars. Within a short time the city of Havana is summed up in one image: the Morro Castle, the gateway to the port of Havana. Sometimes the label has several scenes: the tobacco farm and the Morro Castle with some ships in the distance, for example, linked together by garlands of roses.

Many flowers make up the decorations on the labels, but none quite equals the importance of the rose—carefully cultivated, a symbol of court life,

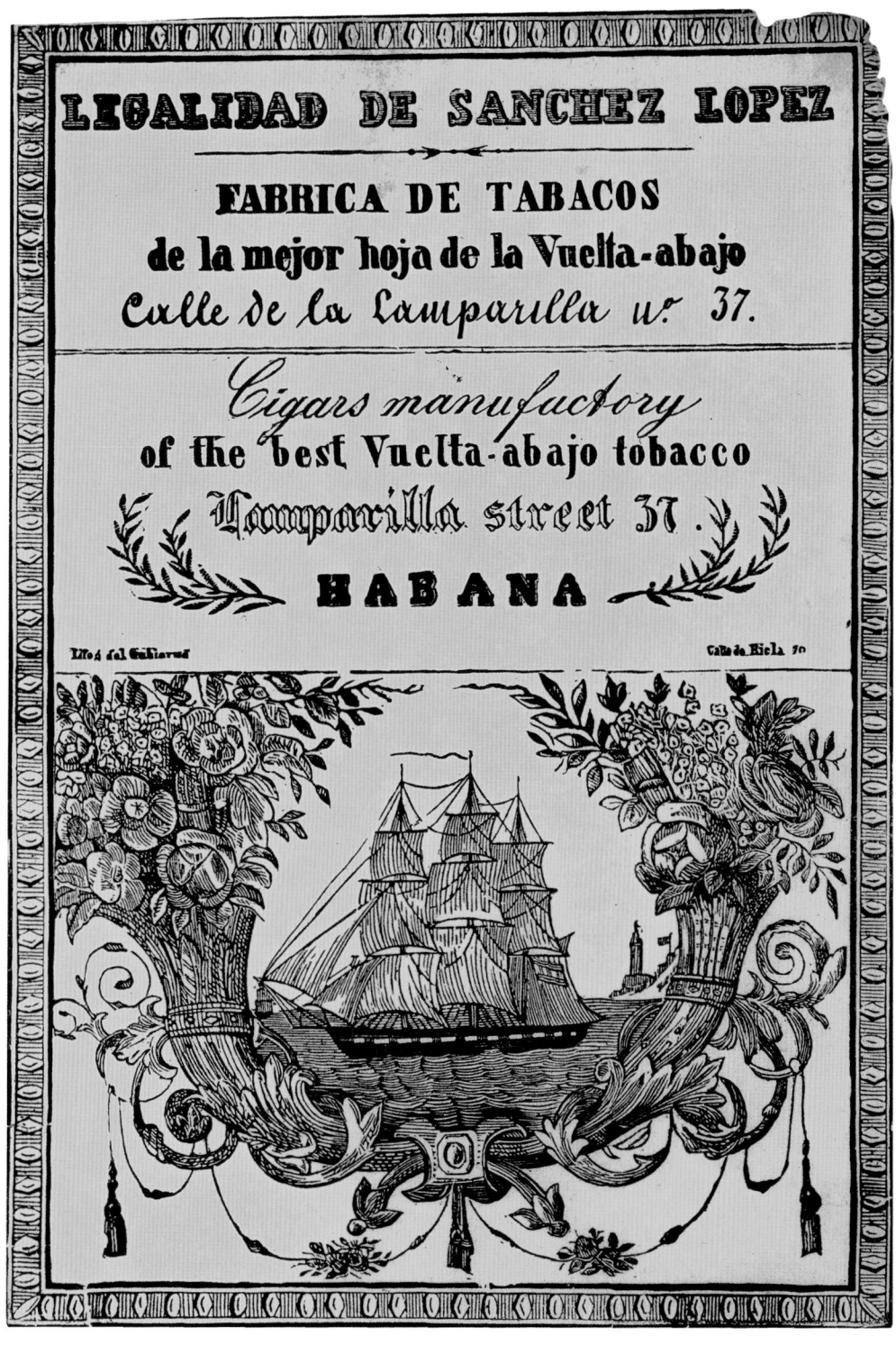

Legalidad, manufactured by Sanchez López, Lamparilla Street No. 37, Havana, produced a label, c. 1860, that shows a ship to indicate its export trade. (Arents Collection, New York Public Library)

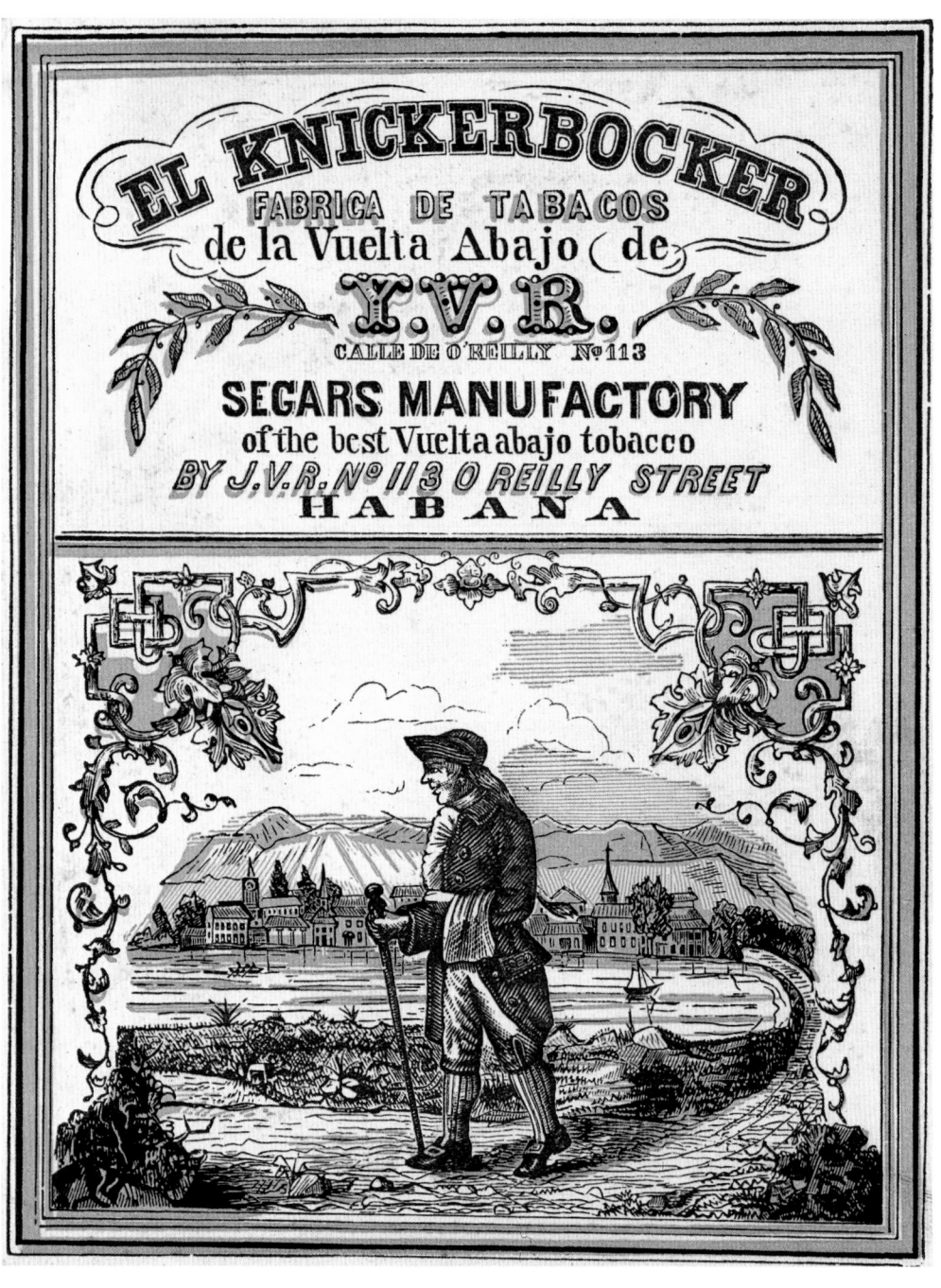

The label for El Knickerbocker cigars, manufactured by J. V. R., O'Reilly Street No. 113, Havana, shows one of the early spellings of "cigars." (Arents Collection, New York Public Library)

and the obsession of gardeners. No other flower is so shockingly aromatic or such a pleasure to the senses—very much like a Havana cigar. Roses were imported from China and gradually made their way into the export trade, and so share a similar history with the cigar. Artists used flowers to join disparate images on a label, to frame the portraits of mysterious women, or soften the image of aggressive brand owners. This is all in the name of the senses—taste more than smell, in fact. A cigar's *flor* (flower) is the product of fermentation, which gives it its characteristic flavor. Interestingly, it is your taste buds that the *flor* is activating.

One of Cuba's most carefully constructed label images is that of the idyllic tobacco factory. Views of the factory were usually arranged around a

central image, like the Morro Castle, or around a character, as in the Punch label. The factory looks like a relaxing place to work, where it was possible to sit down, even wear comfortable felt slippers. The hierarchy of the factory—represented, of course, by the four most highly paid jobs: leaf selection, cigar rolling, cigar sorting, and box decorating—are portrayed in views joined by bunches of flowers. Only men, thin, handsome, and white-skinned, perform these tasks in the ideal factory. There is another side to the story. The myth of the label ignores the vast number of people pressed into the business of producing export cigars. To meet the high demand for the product in the 1850s, women, blacks, prisoners (rolling rooms were called galleries after the big halls in prisons), indentured Chinese, soldiers, and slaves were hired (or hired out) to meet the worldwide demand for cigars. To be fair, cigars were primarily produced in houses, not factories, during the 1850s. Women have always worked in the industry, but until the 1860s they did not work in the large factories and were generally excluded from rolling cigars until recently. Only at the Cohiba factory, founded by Celia Sanchez, were women allowed to enter the industry on all levels. Perhaps, one day, the brand will produce a label with the four power departments pictured on its label entirely staffed by women, surrounding the profile of the brand's Indian head.

Because the consumption of tobacco has always been controversial, it has been important to identify famous people who are proud smokers. George Washington was a prominent tobacco grower; when the Cubans chose his

The 1910 label for Punch cigars, subsequently manufactured by Manuel López, Rayo Street No. 28, Havana, shows the factory as a most congenial place to work. (Collection: The author)

La Señorita Isabel Cubas, manufactured by T and B, Murallia Street No. 27, Havana, were named after a popular ballerina who performed in Latin America and Europe in the 1850s. (Arents Collection, New York Public Library)

name as a label of cigars in the 1840s, it was for that reason and not simply because he was an American president. El Knickerbocker, representing those wonderful buyers from the port of New York, was produced by J.V.R. at 113 O'Reilly Street in Old Havana. Lord Wellington and Napoleon were on labels, as were foppish but popular military officers who smoked cigars. No one could be a more powerful advocate than the brand owner, who would often include his name and portrait on the label. For good measure, the prosperous-looking owners, their images surrounded by ropes of roses, are aided by cupids to arouse desire for these fabulous rolls of tobacco.

In Cuba there is a tradition of having a private stock of cigars prepared at home by women. There are two reasons for this. First, a smoker could have

LA DIANA

HABANA

his own personal blend rolled in exactly the shape of preference, and also it was much cheaper—always a consideration. Leaves could be purchased a few at a time from the houses on Monte Street. Cuban tobacco historian Zoila Lapique says that women also bought leaves from factories for home rolling. She remembers from her childhood the smell of her father, the room where he smoked, the coat he wore, and the preparation of his cigars. Nineteenth-century cigar labels pictured the people who ideally rolled them for you: your wife, daughter, or sweetheart. These labels feature classic faces of Andalusian or Galician women, and sometimes faces of very young girls. Adelaid, Camila, Isabel, and Amelia are the brand names. Famous women, like Señorita Isabel Cubas, the ballerina who performed in Europe and Latin America, are rare.

Travelers' accounts suggest that everybody in Cuba smoked, but it is unclear if cigars were actually being marketed to women. The Belle Epoque with its Knowing Women, Bohemian Women, and Sports Women, came much later and are not characteristic of Havana labels. There are no naked women on Havana cigar labels, not even camouflaged as artistic nudes, though there may have been tiny pictures, inserted in cigar boxes and easily removed, that were quasi-erotic.

Nor are there black women on the labels, though they were often mistresses in Spanish Cuba. No wife wanted to think about that famous threat, the second family. The brand owners knew that a box of cigars cannot alienate

La Diana cigars, manufactured by Julian Alvarez y Hermanos, San Nicolas Street No. 120, Havana, produced a label, c. 1865, with two of the most popular images: roses and a young girl. (Collection: Alberto Bustamante)

CABANAS

PRIZE MEDAL of the EXHIBITION LONDON 1851

FABRICA
DE TABACOS DE LA HIJA DE CABAÑAS Y CARBAJAL

*Calle de la Lamparilla haciendo esquina á la de
S. Ignacio ó sea de Volcan número 92.*

DE SEGUNDA CLASE.—*Carvajal.*

HABANA.

Another popular image for cigar labels, seen in one c. 1859 for Cabanas, manufactured by Cabanas y Carbajal, Lamparilla and San Ignacio Streets, Havana, depicts classically rendered images. (Arents Collection, New York Public Library)

women: it must be made welcome in the house, beautifully designed to be placed in libraries, drawing rooms, and dining rooms. No mulattas are featured on these labels, either. Cigarettes (referred to as "dirty" since they contain scraps of tobacco alluded to as floor sweepings from the cigar factory, and "little deaths" by Cubans who understand the danger of the quick, hot burn) had labels that used demeaning imagery—lazy blacks, blacks dressed as Indians, and mistresses of all types—for marketing. Cigars, never! Conservative respectability, at least on the surface, and extremely expensive packaging sold this luxury item. I think that the forerunner of the cigar label is the enamel snuff box, with its beautiful portraits and pastoral views, glassy surface and gilding, once used by men and women alike.

FABRICA DE TABACOS

DE

H. UPMANN

HABANA

This is my Signature.

TRADE MARK REGISTERED

"MADE IN HAVANA-CUBA"

The factory owners of the independent brands were competitive, vying for world recognition. Since 1851, when Cabañas and Carvajal received the premiere medal for their cigars at Queen Victoria's Great Exhibition in London, medals had become the equivalent of industrial trophies, and representations of the medals showed up on labels. From that time on the up-and-coming factory owners competed at world expositions, and medals became an especially important endorsement for the independents Romeo y Julieta, and H. Upmann, who turned his label into a trophy case.

Cigar labels are part of the reconstructed romance of Cuba's history. Some of these labels look like illustrated children's books. The Intrepido label shows Columbus standing with one hand on an anchor. Seated before him on a rock

Medals were eagerly sought at international expositions as this label, c. 1900, for H. Upmann proudly shows. (Collection: Alberto Bustamante)

POR LARRAÑAGA

MARCA INDEPENDIENTE DE TABACOS DE VUELTA ABAJO.

LARRAÑAGA

A label, c. 1900, for Por Larrañaga cigars, manufactured by Antonio López, Belascoain No. 2, Havana, shows La India dressed as a goddess riding a chariot. (Collection: Alberto Bustamante)

and looking up to him is *La India Habana*. The shield of Havana, the key and three castles, is present, as are the ubiquitous roses. Here is the intrepid sea voyager, with his ship in the distance. One label is called El Mapamundi, which refers to the world map that was drawn in 1500 by Juan de la Cosa, who accompanied Columbus on his first voyage. The label of La Legítimidad Real Fábrica de F.P. Del Río y Ca. shows Columbus kneeling before the Catholic monarchs Isabella and Ferdinand, and the artist has managed to include Indians attending the event. On the El Nuevo Mundo label of Angel Ramirez, Columbus is in a circle surrounded by male and female Indians wearing colorful feathers.

By the time the Havana factory owners were actively marketing their cigars, in the 1820s, it had been two centuries since the Indians were nearly eradicated. The owners tested images of several different Indians, and finally settled on La India, a European woman, to represent them. She is a beautiful

The Flor de Alvarez label, c. 1900, for cigars produced by J. Alvarez and Co., Estrella No. 100, Havana. (Collection: Alberto Bustamante)

woman with a crown of multicolored feathers, usually wearing only gold jewelry, a short skirt made of a few well-chosen feathers, and thong sandals with straps running up her legs. A similar representation had been selling America to the French for over a century, appearing, for example, on map cartouches and Sevres porcelain. The Cubans appropriated this European image to represent their tobacco. Por Larrañaga shows her dressed as a goddess riding in a chariot pulled by lions—probably British lions, the big buyers. She is accompanied by cherubs in regional headdresses who assist her in bringing the cigars to patrons all over the world.

The label of El Rey del Mundo, The King of the World, features an androgynous La India, without breasts, riding in a chariot pulled by animals with labels around their necks. Animals represent the world: a horse (Europe), an elephant (Asia), a camel (Africa), a mule (America), and a sheep (Oceania). The Morro Castle is in the background, tobacco plants frame the Spanish

The Mapamundi label refers to the world map drawn in 1500 by Juan de la Cosa, who accompanied Columbus on his first voyage. (Collection: Alberto Bustamante)

crest, and cigars in bundles and boxes, and tobacco in barrels and bales lay at the picture's edge. Nothing could be sillier, but this label is still in existence and has been surprisingly successful.

Inevitably there were changes on the labels during the years of foreign ownership. Most notable is the lack of Havana street addresses, since some of the cigars were manufactured outside the country. So much leaf tobacco was being shipped out of the country that stemming factories were set up in Cuba to reduce the shipping weight and tariffs.

Today the New Indian is used to symbolize a pristine time before the European discovery of tobacco. To Cubans it is quite simple: the natives first discovered this mysterious plant, and since the 1960s the use of an Indian's head on the Cohiba cigar has signaled a new ownership, a repossession of tobacco, a new identity with the Indians' history, and a fresh start. Other

products, such as beer, had been marketed successfully using an Indian logo, so it was probably thought to be a sound choice, as well as a bit nostalgic.

Havana cigar labels tell very clear stories; though they are constructed fictions based on murky history, these advertising stories stem from a clear conviction of truth, and are therefore good marketing symbols. Europeans admire them for the quality of their lithography and the fine application of gold and bronze leaf, which is both beautiful and amazing, and collect them as novelties for these reasons. Collectors sometimes forget that there was a hard-won difference between Cuban labels and their imitations. Knockoffs of Havana cigar labels were common worldwide, so much so that some Havana cigar companies had lithography shops within their factories, and all went to great lengths to control their manufacture. Even today, large safes in the box decorating room hold the factory labels. To Cubans, cigar labels are popular art.

The label for La Legítimidad cigars, manufactured by F. P. Del Río y Ca., Figuras Street No. 28, 30, and 32, Havana, shows Columbus kneeling before Queen Isabella and King Ferdinand of Spain. (Collection: Alberto Bustamante)

"FONSECA" CIGARS DE LUXE.

THE BOX

Havana exporters began to package their product in boxes in about 1859. Boxes of fifty, a hundred, or five hundred cigars joined the traditional bundles. There is conflicting information regarding the initiator of the cigar box, and nothing regarding its origin. In speculating about the history of the box, we should remember that Havana had been the port from which all commodities found in the Indies were shipped. Wrapping, boxing, and shipping from the port of Havana began as early as 1492, and included everything from perishable fruits to gold artifacts from the Americas. Nearly everything must have been boxed or crated. The entire handwritten documentation of the Spanish conquest and the colonization of New Spain, for example, had been packaged and exported to the archives in Seville and Madrid; to look at an original Spanish manuscript sent from Havana is to experience layers of wrappers and yards of string, and is a study in seals, flourishes of the pen, and signatures. *Habaneros* were sophisticated packagers, no doubt about it.

Could it be possible that information about Commodore Perry's trip to Japan in 1853, which enthralled Europeans and Americans and greatly influenced the decorative arts, might have reached Havana in the form of boxes, perhaps wooden tea chests, made of thin wood and sealed around the edges

Facing page: Habaneros have a long and fascinating tradition of sophisticated packaging. This collection of antique cigar boxes is at the Tobacco Museum in Havana.

The Fonseca factory wrapped its cigars in Japanese paper which could be inscribed with a personal logo. This 1910 display (*above*) was published in William Gill's *Havana Cigars,* of 1910.

with metal bands? At precisely the same time the rest of the world suddenly adopted Japanese detailing, Havana cigar exporters started making cedar boxes with hinged lids, sealed and decorated with strips of paper that covered the nail holes. These boxes were filled with rows of cigars and the label, a little picture previously fastened to a barrel lid, was now safely inside. A world of possibilities for marketing and retailing opened up with the box.

The Cubans were trying to market a hand-assembled product and refine its packaging to give the product further uniformity and a greater sense of precision. Uniformity implies that each cigar is going to taste just as good as the last one, and that there are no disappointments in the group. The box also made forgeries difficult. Bundles of cigars, with only one label on a barrel, were a bit more ambiguous, the origin only verbally confirmed. Sealed boxes, precisely labeled, carrying an exact Havana address, eliminated some of the forgeries and problems of questionable authenticity.

The Fonseca factory wrapped its cigars in foil, then in Japanese paper which could be inscribed, upon order, with a private logo. The New York Yacht Club and the Metropolitan Club purchased these "deluxe" cigars. In his 1910 *Havana Cigars,* William Gill called F. E. Fonseca the artist of the cigar industry: "Fully 60 percent of the Fonseca production is used at receptions, banquets, conventions, and for presents and souvenirs, and this brand of cigar is so exclusive that it will be found only in the finest clubs and in the homes of those who love good things." Fonseca must have bypassed the retailers with direct orders from the factory.

The box made cigars market-ready. All the retailer had to do was pry open the lid and the rest was up to the buyer. Tobacco historian Carl Avery Werner, writing for Tobacco Leaf Publishing in 1922, asserted that by 1900 you could buy cigars in grocery stores; barbershops; shoeshining establishments; fruit, candy, and beverage stands; billiard rooms; restaurants; railroad trains; department stores; and hotels, as well as in the tobacco stores. Werner offered a word of advice to cigar store managers: "Suggest, but don't argue. You know very well that smoking is one-half imagination. Allow for it."

Filetes (*facing page*), strips of decorative paper used to form an ornamental edge for cigar boxes, and rings (*above*) are still used in the Havana factories.

Overleaf: A smoker enjoys his cigar *al fresco* in the Casablanca neighborhood of Havana.

SMOKING
AND
PARAPHERNALIA

Cigars, especially big cigars, have always been a symbol of power. But no matter how important you are, or how expensive the cigar, etiquette requires offering a cigar to everyone in the party. It is a social obligation. Cigars celebrate the birth of a baby, winning an election, success of a racehorse, and triumph over everyday life.

Most Cuban cigar cases hold three cigars. Three cigars in the breast pocket symbolize yourself, your friend, and another. At the Museum of the City of Havana there are cigars from the battlefield wrapped in plantain leaves (no doubt inspired by the *Cartilla Rústica*), cases hand-fashioned in leather, and a silver case that belonged to the brother of Antonio Maceo, the great African-Cuban general.

Cubans are lucky if three cigars are available, unless you work in a cigar factory where it is possible to smoke all day. Today, during this period of austerity, when as many cigars are exported as possible, the number and quality of cigars available to Cubans is greatly reduced. Cubans can buy cheap two peso cigars from rollers who prepare cigars right in their houses. The government in Havana Province issues a little breva called El Cacique, named after an Indian chief, and Selectos, which are sold in some bodegas and can be bought with the *libreta* (ration card), four per month. The Pita, rolled at the Heroes del Moncada, is a rare gift cigar. In Manicaragua, the government breva is called Reloba, and in Pinar del Rio, Serbio. The tobacco in these cigars has been rejected for export cigars: if you open up one of these cigars, the color of the tobacco is inconsistent, and often the filler is made up of many pieces. However, since there are sympathetic and skillful people in cigar factories throughout Cuba, a few good cigars are made under these conditions.

Smoking a *habano* export cigar, however, is out of the question, and many old cigar smokers have simply given up smoking.

Raul Corrales used to smoke Cazadores, which he described as large and very strong, and H. Upmann No. 4s. He bought these in bundles of twenty-five, and smoked twelve a day. Storing them was not a concern since he smoked the bundle in two days. This was the normal pattern in prerevolutionary Cuba when smokers smoked eight, twelve, or fifteen a day. Their children remember closets, drawers, and cabinets filled with cigars. Roland Sainz, a New York gallery owner, remembers that his father had a desk drawer lined with cedar, and every week a man arrived to fill it. In Havana I asked his father about the desk drawer, and a smile spread across his face. "I imported all my cigars from Manicaragua." His wife produced a large cedar box with "Cazadores by Bauza," a famous prerevolutionary factory in Santa Clara Province, engraved inside the lid, saying that it had been a company gift many years ago. I asked him when and where he had smoked his cigars, and his wife answered. "First, he drank coffee, then he had breakfast, and then he smoked a cigar. He worked in an office, so he smoked there after his morning coffee, after lunch, after the afternoon coffee at three, one in the late afternoon, after dinner, and at night." As she spoke she held up her fingers and had counted seven cigars. She continued, "The other cigars were smoked while working and during business conversations. He smoked at least twelve a day." I asked his wife if she smoked, and she rolled her eyes and said that there had been enough smoke.

A miscellany of accesories, such as this three-cigar pocket case, has emerged to complement the *habano*. (Collection: Tobacco Museum, Havana)

The Tobacco Museum in Havana has cabinets full of commemorative cigars, tobacco art, and cigar boxes (*facing page*).

Overleaf: The *habano* is a pleasure that is enjoyed by both old and young, men and women, in Havana.

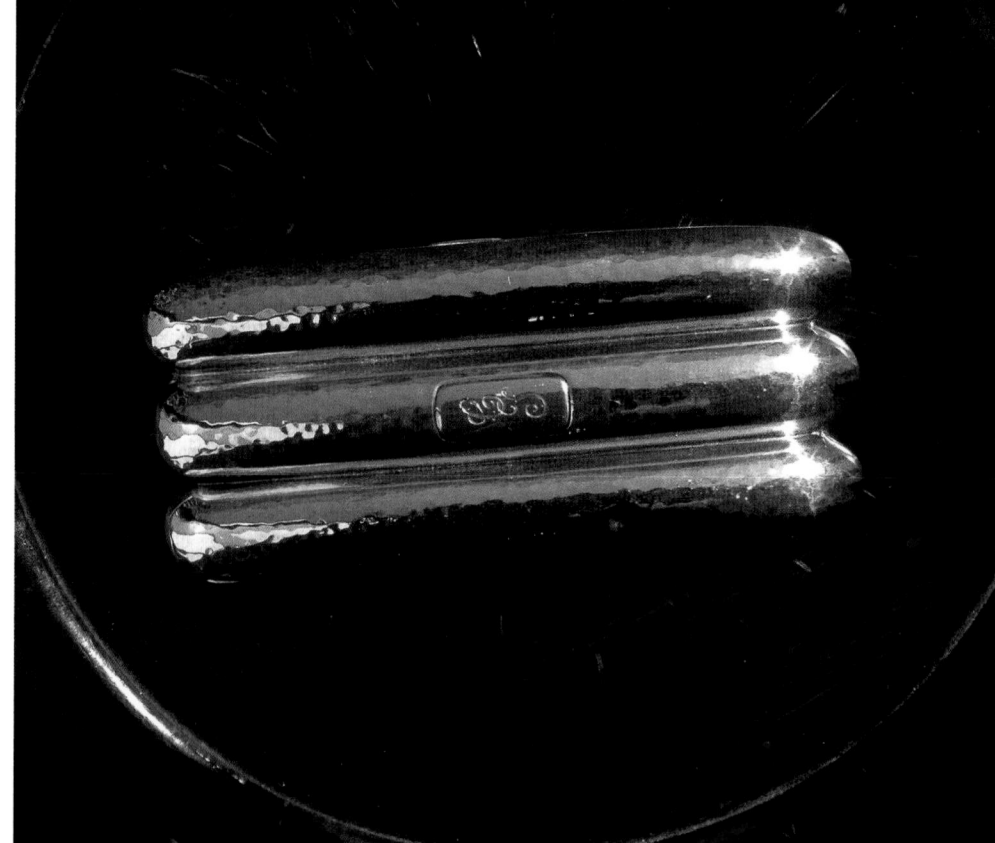

Samuel Hazard writes that Cubans are very particular about preserving the natural aroma of their cigars and keep them wrapped in "oiled and soft silk." Perhaps there is a new role for expensive scarves, and a beautiful, well-kept young woman will be pictured on a label with a few Havana cigars wrapped in her scarf and tucked into her purse. Present-day Cuba is about as remote from a Hermès scarf as you can get, yet Cubans are secure in the knowledge that they hold the key to a world-class luxury product—their cigars.

COMMEMORATIVE CIGARS

In Cuba, special commemorative cigars are kept behind glass. There are cigars often measuring eighteen to twenty-four inches long, placed in glass-fronted cabinets along with porcelain figurines. The Cabañas cigars sent to London in 1851, which brought the country so much prestige, are also preserved under glass. The cigar sent into outer space aboard the Cuban-Soviet space flight, appropriately, is housed in a glass capsule. It is decorated with a single red star, like the one on Che's beret, a symbol of the country. There is also a Cuban folk art of making portraits from tobacco leaves, and these extremely fragile pieces of tobacco are pressed between pieces of glass and displayed.

The commemorative cigar has long been a treasured keepsake among Cubans. This one, shown here full size, was specially manufactured for the dinner celebrating the 30th anniversary of the Cohiba cigar factory.

Tobacco jars have been used as a marketing device in apothecary shops since the sixteenth century. This Partagás jar dates from the nineteenth century. (Collection: Tobacco Museum, Havana)

JARS

From the sixteenth century to the present, cigars stored in porcelain jars have been sold in apothecary shops and drugstores. Jars have been used, like the boxes, as a marketing device, though they are somewhat fragile for shipping, usually only for special cigars by Partagás and H. Upmann.

THE STORY OF THE CIGAR-STORE INDIAN

The cigar-store Indian, although it surely sold tobacco, is not really so much a part of the marketing of the Havana cigar as one might think, but the story is interesting nonetheless. The Indian was used from the 1600s to around 1900 to sell tobacco. A carved figure was placed in the window or just outside an establishment to indicate that tobacco was sold within. The earliest recorded use of the Indian as a store sign is 1617, in an engraving published in Brathwait's *Smoking Age*. In it, the Indian, smoking a huge roll of tobacco, is displayed in a London apothecary shop window. This method of marketing was later copied by seventeenth-century tobacconists, when, Werner explains, tobacco was regarded as a gift from the native to whites. English shopkeepers continued to adopt the marketing strategy, but changed the characters: baseball players, plantation Negroes, and Punch, a distinctly British character, were all enlisted to promote tobacco sales.

DISHES

In Havana there are a few cigar dishes. Well-laid Victorian tables had cigar holders at various intervals among the fruit compotes, cakestands, and sugar jars. They are shaped like baskets with handles, made of wire or porcelain, and hold four or six cigars. It is easy to imagine cigars rolled by wives and daughters, placed on a tray with morning coffee for husbands and fathers, or maybe to smoke with women friends.

The cigar dish was a standard accoutrement of the well-laid Victorian table; this porcelain one held several cigars and would be offered around after dinner. (Collection: Tobacco Museum, Havana)

MEMENTOES

Speaking to anthropologist Miguel Barnet about his own books based on interviews, I thought he might be able to tell me something about tobacco. Like all Cubans I had interviewed, he recalled his family when I asked about cigars.

"My grandmother smoked cigars. Her family and my great-grandfather's family were tobacco growers in Pinar del Rio." They had left Cuba and opened a factory in Tampa to escape the violence of the War of Independence, but returned in 1902 when the war ended. During the next fifty years,

Barnet said, members of his family moved to California, New York, and New Jersey.

"My grandmother moved out of the big family house to an apartment in the Vedado section of Havana and grew old there." She continued to smoke cigars from Pinar del Rio sent by family friends who were tobacco growers in the Vuelta Abajo region, or ordered boxes of Por Larrañagas from the factory on Carlos III Street. "My brother and father and I were the only others still living in Cuba, so we all visited her. She remained very bright and very healthy, and lived to be ninety-five years old, still smoking cigars."

One day he received a telephone call from his father asking him to come quickly and to bring a doctor. "When we arrived she was slumped over in her chair. She had always been so bright and alert, and now she had a dull look in her eyes and even a little spittle on her chin." After a time she roused, looked at all those assembled, smiled a little, and asked for coffee. "She drank the coffee and then asked for a cigar. She puffed on the cigar and even brought it to her lips a few times. She seemed to enjoy it. Then she fell back and was dead. We took the cigar and put a piece of glass over it. We've kept it as the last cigar."

This gold and enamel Cartier New York "cigar band" ring (*above*), dating from 1971, makes a luxurious gift for the cigar aficianado who has everything. (Collection: Lucy Scott)

Whether because of the scarcity of luxury items or simply common preference, most Cubans eschew the use of cigar cutters, such as this one engraved FIDEL CASTRO RUZ (*below*), in favor of using their teeth. (Tobacco Museum, Havana)

TOOLS

Treatises on cigar smoking do not even mention biting the head off the cigar before lighting it, but in Havana it is rarely done otherwise. Looking back, I believe that only people who feel they represent the industry use a cutter. In the factory the curved knife, the *chaveta*, is on everybody's table, so it is second nature to use it to cut the end. Some cigar rollers, like Esther at the Romeo y Julieta factory, finish the head the old-fashioned way, with a little twist—easy to nip off with the teeth. Some people remember their parents using scissors or other tools. The Tobacco Museum has a few dented and clearly well-used silver cigar tools. Luxury items have been in such short supply in Cuba that it is possible that cigar tools and cutters are simply not practical to

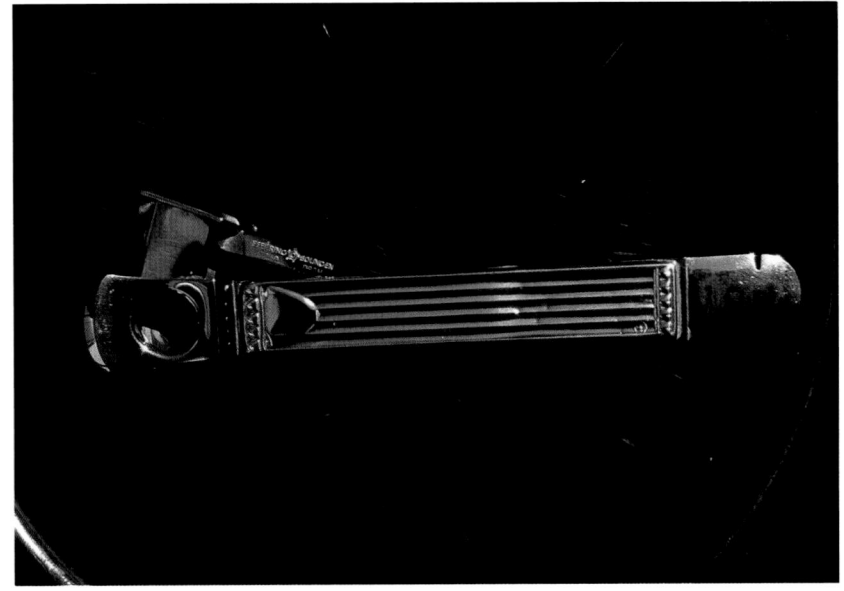

replace when they wear out, but I believe that most Cubans have always preferred to use their teeth.

F. W. Fairholt's book, *Tobacco: Its History and Associations,* published in 1859, pictures a cigar cutter which he says was designed in Berlin. It is a pocket knife with a hole for the cigar tip in the outer casing. When the knife is pressed down, the blade does the job. The cutter has a small side box to hold matches.

The matchbox, called a cigar light, was designed to occupy very little space in the pocket. The English, those great cigar enthusiasts, put Punch and other advertising scenes such as hunting on their matchboxes. Today, cedar matches are the light of choice in Havana, and lighted cedar strips are considered the best way to light a cigar. In the factory stores, the managers suggest using a cedar strip torn from the sheet between the layers of cigars in a box; this provides a light with no odor or taste.

Proper lighting is a serious issue. In Havana, everyone knows that if the cigar goes out, it must be relit immediately. If there is a change in the temperature of the tobacco, the taste changes as well. Smoking fresh cigars (recently rolled and unaged) in a humid climate requires attention and commitment. Cubans believe the cigar must be respected, and the smoker should make an effort not to contaminate the flavor or the aroma and to make a good light.

THE CANDELA

Hazard writes that the *candela*, a silver or plated dish or vase filled with wood ashes, "in which lies buried a live coal or two," was used to light after-dinner cigars. He said that in the nineteenth century it would be brought to the table just as regularly as any other dish, and is the most pleasing way to light one's cigar, better than an odorous match.

A proper light is serious business, as these early nineteenth-century English box covers for "cigar lights," or matchboxes, attest. (Arents Collection, New York Public Library)

The offering

I was often told in Cuba by those who practiced Santería that cigars are lighted for the spirits. For example, every Monday, several people assured me, they light a candle and a cigar for the deity Elegguá. Tomás Fernandez Robaina, author of *Hablen Paleros y Santeros*, a series of interviews with Bantu (*Paleros*) and Yoruban (*Santeros*) religious practitioners, explained, "Lighting a cigar is not part of African ritualism, but is a Cuban invention. For Afro-Cubans, cigars celebrate the influence of the aboriginals on the slaves. So, for us, it is all the more important to preserve the ritual." He recounted the history of the shiploads of African slaves sent to Cuba, some of whom escaped to the forests of Cuba and became runaways called maroons. There they adopted the beliefs of the Indians.

Candelas, such as this one dating from 1860, were used to light after-dinner cigars. (Collection: The Silver Museum, Havana)

Overleaf: La Tropical beer garden, edged by the Almendares River, provides a peaceful retreat in which to enjoy the *habano*.

"Blacks learned from the Indians how to run away from white people. We must cherish this. It is not only about freedom from slavery. To smoke is to offer thanks. It brings a kind of spiritual protection." I thought about the cigars I'd seen at the Santería botanical stall on Infanta Street and remembered the opening scene in Tomás Gutierrez Alea's last film, *Guantanamera*, where a truck driver blows rum and cigar smoke on all sixteen wheels of his rig before taking off for Havana.

Robaina went on to explain that in the work of the *Santeros*, cigars are one factor in the communication between the people and the spirits of the dead.

Practitioners of Santería include cigars, which are lit for spirits, among their ceremonial items, such as these for sale on Infanta Street in Central Havana.

"When they descend from heaven, which could happen at any time, they want to smoke, and so cigars must be ready for them." I asked where everyone gets the cigars. He conceded, "In these tough times even a part of the ashes will do."

ASHTRAYS

Surprisingly, I'd seen very few ashtrays in this nation of cigar smokers. Perhaps the fine particles of ash, turned to dust, were simply swept and mopped from tile floors daily. However, I had seen one big ashtray when I'd visited the office of Eusebio Leal, the Historian of the City. In the center of the big glass ashtray was the seal of the United States Senate.

Rooms in Havana are perfect for cigar smoking. Ceilings are uncommonly high, and only windows in modern buildings contain glass. Smoke simply rises; breezes refresh the air. The old private houses are one story, with enormous floor-to-ceiling windows grated with strong iron bars studded with florettes and softened by curlicues, never curtained, and facing the street. Curious travelers out at night, catching the aroma of a cigar, can stare shamelessly into a room. These are often lovely spaces, floored and wainscotted in tiles, hung with chandeliers, and often connected to a room beyond by an open archway. The smoker, usually sitting by a small lamp that highlights the profile of his face and the cigar, or illuminated by the screen of a television showing the nightly *novela*, puffs while smoke floats toward the rafters.

The most famous room in Havana, the cabaret room at the Tropicana nightclub, is covered only by the sky. It is walled in mirrors, lighted with neon, furnished with royal palms and stands of bamboo, and graced with fabulously dressed dancing girls. On February 28, 1997, the room was filled with about seven hundred cigar smokers gathered to celebrate the 30th anniversary of the founding of the Cohiba cigar factory. After dinner (but before the arrival of Fidel) we were offered robustos, and, for a few minutes, even this room became smoke-filled.

The huge and elegant reading room at the José Martí National Library has marble-faced walls and windows filled by horizontal louvers just under the roofline. Shafts of light shine through the louvers but never really reach the floor. Everything else—hundreds of oak drawers containing the card catalog, rows of readers sitting at long wooden tables—is in shadow. A bird had managed to get into the room and was flying about, looking for an exit, but the ceiling was so high and the room so large that no one was distracted. At least no one else seemed to be watching. It was at that moment that I became aware that someone was smoking a cigar in the reading room. I was a little shocked, smelling the smoke before I saw the smoker, and I turned to look as he strolled by my table to the other end of the room. The rest of us, denim-clad readers and staff, grandiose in our pursuits, suddenly became very ordinary. The cigar smoker, wearing a midnight-blue, double-breasted suit with an open-collared white shirt, was tall and slender, with dark skin. For the next hour or so, I watched the tailored shoulders shift ever so slightly before I smelled a new infusion of the lovely fragrance of the *habano*. I don't remember what I read that day, only the silvery spiral up into the sunlight and bird flight of the interior sky above. *¡Nace Habana, soy habanera . . . y fume habanos, aché!*

Overleaf: Santería dieties, depicted here painted on wooden plaques for sale in Old Havana's Cathedral Plaza, are believed to want to smoke cigars when they visit the corporeal realm.

DIRECTORY OF HAVANA CIGAR FACTORIES

TABAQUERIAS DE LA HABANA, 1840
FROM THE *DIRECTORIO DE LA CIUDAD DE LA HABANA Y ESTRAMUROS* BY EDUARDO JONES
HAVANA, 1840.

c = comerciante
f = fabricante
alm. tab. = almacen de tobaco

Acosta, Pedro (f), Monte 132.
Acosta, Antonio (c), Monte 214.
Acosta, Manuel, Sitios 31.
Acosta, Desiderio (c), Monte 292.
Acebal, Bernardo (c), Aguiar 70.
Adraz, Gregorio, Antonmoco 36.
Aguilar, Luis, Gloria 0
Aguila, Pedro (c), Damas 35
Aguado, Joaquin (c), Sol 60
Alcedo, Domingo (c), Monte 95
Alrey, Pedro, Habana 63
Alvarez, Jose (c), Maloja 72
Alvarez, Jose (c), Pena Blanca 7
Alvarez, Nicolas (c), Monte 95
Alvarez, Jose, San Juan 15
Alvarez, Juan, San Antonio 3
Alvarez, Jose (c), Maloja 73
Alvarez, Domingo (c), Animas 38
Alvarez, Domingo, Monte 2
Alvarez, Pedro (c), Monte 301 (alm. tab.)
Alcaros, Miguel, Inquisidor 73
Alcantara, Jose, Corral 29
Alamillo, Jose (c), Neptuno 104
Alsido, Domingo (c), Monte 95
Amador, Pedro (f), Mision 3
Amenter, Lucio (c), Obrapia 36
Angel, Pedro (c), Antonmoco 35
Ariosa, Francisco de (c), Acosta 103
Arambrat, Ortuno, Bernaza 0
Arena, Calisto (c), Manrique 60
Arrianda, Juan (c), Monte 63 (alm. tab.)
Apolonio, Jose Cruz (c), Corral 139
Aparicio, Fernando (c), J. del Monte 69
Aparicio, Antonio (c), C. del Junco 18
Avalo, Antonio (c), Salud 51
Arnau, Felix (c), Monte 255
Aguety, Salvador (c), Esperanza 7

Barrero, Jose (c), Jesus Maria 106
Baroega, Luis (c), S. Salvador 5
B., Jose (c), Oficios 11
Banos, Ramon (c), Bernaza 22
Batista, Maximo (c), Neptuno 56
Barroso, Juan B., San Miguel 131
Barzat, Juan (c), Curazao 26
Beyla, Agustin (c), San Miguel 77

Brito, Juan (c), San Lazaro 22
Bronz, Carlos (c), Salud 102
Bosques, Manuel (c), San Nicolas 7
Bolano, Jose (c), Prado 15

Castillo, Gavino del (c), Penalver 34
Castillo, Miguel del (c), Horcon 172
Castillo, Jose (c), Jesus del Monte 26
Castillo, Miguel (c), Jesus Maria 77
Castillo, Jose Maria (c), Monte 54
Castro, Jose Fernandez (f), Obispo 6
Castro, Jose Fernandez (f), Obrapia
Castro, Jose Fernandez (f), O'Reilly 151
Castro, Jose Fernandez (f), O'Reilly 25
Castro, Juan (tlab), Acosta 80
Cabrera, Jose de la Luz (c), Monte 302
Cabrera, Joaquin (c), Crespo 26
Cardenas, Joaquin, Sitios 115
Casas, Francisco (c), Angeles 50
Cau, Pilar, Angeles 28
Camara, Juan de la (c), Dragones 4
Casanova, Sebastian (c), Rayo 38
Carezjal, Manuel (c), Lamparilla 92
Cabanes, Baltasar (c), Obispo 31
Cariaga, Ignacio (c), Monte 79
Cosido, Gregario (f), Monte 249 (alm. tab.)
Cos, Antonio (c), Monte 217
Contreras, Macario (c), Salud 1
Carrasco, Juan (c), Jesus del Monte 108
Castillar, clemente (c), Mercaderes 2
C., Felipe (c), Horqueta 34
Chapu, Felix (c), Maloja 23
Ciriel, Rafael, Corral 139
Cristo, Ramon (c), Sitios--
Crespo, Bernardino (c), Corral 18
Cruz, Jose (c), Pte. de Maboa 93
Cueto, Manuel (c), Gurazao 26 1/2
Cubney, Juan (c), Obispo 56
Cueva, Francisco (c), Vives 20
Conico, Juan (c), Pza. del Cristo 38
Consuegra, Miguel, Pza. del Cristo 19
Conde, Juan (c), Economico 59

Diaz, Esteban Domingo (c), Sol 60
Diaz, Santos (c), Rayo 39
Diaz, Jose (c), Monte 134
Diaz, Jose (c), Animas 25
Diaz, Narciso (c), ...17

Escral, Geronimo (c), Monte 15
Esmar, Pablo (c), Horqueta 13
Esquinaldo, Francisco (vda.), Maloja--

Fernandez, Juan (c), Crespo 66
Fernandez, Antonio (c), Salud 37
Fontana, Joaquin (c), Monte 29

Fors, Jose (c), San Ignacio 89
Flores, Jose A. (c), Sol 82
Fervan, Jose (c), P. de Alfaro 21
Fustier y Comp. (c), San Salvador de Hor 1

Galan, Juan B. (c), Monte 163
Garcia, Manuel (c), Maloja 73
Gonzalez, Jose (c), Monte 92
Gonzalez, Justo (c), Pte. Maboa--
Gonzalez, Antonio (c), O'Reilly 46
Garcia Espinosa, Juan (c), P. del Vapor 45
Gueso, Juana, Rayo 25
Gueradiaga, Jose M. (f), Baratillo 99

Hernandez, Jose de Luz (c), San Lazaro 9
Hernandez, Facundo (c), Habana 132
Hernandez, Domingo (c), Aguila 20
Hernandez, Vicente (c), Sitios 45
Hernandez, Pablo (c), Monte 85
Hernandez, Jose (c), Monte 85
Herrera, Manuel (c),, Aguiar 31
Hensel, Henrique (c), Aguila 20

Iglesias, Jacobo (c), Obispo 5
Izquierdo, Santiago (c), Monte 80

Jimenez, Felipe (c), Concordia 61
Jimenez, Joaquin (c), Angeles 6
Jimenez, Narciso (c), Consulado 19

Leal, Jose C. (c), Empedrado 67
Lechasaba, Carlos (c), San Lazaro 31
Lapuente, Jaime (c), Obispo 102
Lerezma, Lucas (c), Teniente Rey 12
Loizaga, Joaquin (c), San Ignacio 105
Lopez, Manuel (c), Horqueta 34
Lopez, Francisco (c), Monte 231
Lopez, Antonio (c), Jesus del Monte--
Lopez, Felipe (c), Aguila--

Martinez, Julian (c), Neptuno 115
Martinez, Cayetano (c)< San Lazaro 57
Marquett, J.R. (c), San Miguel 142
Mason, Andres (c), Empedrado 90
Mata, Juan de (c), Curazao 23
Mano, Cipriano (c), Manrique 87
Marin, Fidel (c), Amargura 72
Miranda, Felix, Habana 70
Mora, Antonio, Jesus del Monte--
Montero, Rafael (c), Horqueta 124
Moyer, Carlos (c), Oficios 9
Mier Perez, Manuel (c), Villegas 31
Montero, E. (c), Amargura 89
Munoz, Rafael, Obispo 6

Noriega, Pablo (c), Campanario--

Olivo, Enrique (c), S. L. Gonzaga 32

Padron, Lazaro (c), Amargura 46
Paricio, Florencio (c), Cuba--
Palinar, Carlos (c), Monte 114
Palomino, Jose (c), Concordia 84
Padilla, Jose (cocinero), Monte 209
Padura, Alejandro (c), San Rafael 105
Perez, Juan (c), Monte 174
Perez, Joaquin (c), Villano 12
Perez, Francisco M. (c), Aguacate 76
Perez, Geronimo (c), Oficios 35
Perez, Manuel (c), Horqueta 34
Plasencio, Santiago (c), San Nicolas 63
Perero, Jose (c), Crespo 61
Perrero, Jose (c), Salud 63
Polo, Isidro (c), San Nicolas 63
Puente, Santiago (c), Sol 14
Pujata, Francisco (c), Monte 45

Pluma, Agustin (c), Rayo 15

Quintero, Gabriel (c), Angeles 24

Rea, Jose de la (c), Farruco 17
Rencurrel, Jose (c), Muralla 33
Pendon, Juan N. (c), Manrique 49
Redondo, Manuel (c), Amargura 10
Ribero, Tomas (c), Monte 15
Ribero, Antonio (cocinero), San Ignacio 69
Ribero, Ramon (c), Penalver 30
Ribero, Tomas (c), Monte 319
Rivas, Manuel (c), Monte 78
Rodriguez, Andres (c), O'Reilly 128
Rodriguez, Bernardo (zapatero), Lealtad--
Rodriguez, Jose (c), San Lazaro 305
Rojas, Jose A. (c), Jesus del Monte 68
Rojas, Ramon (c), San Nicolas 60
Roldan, Domingo (c), Rayo 41
Rosales, Tomas, Animas 9
Ruiz, Manuel, Empedrado 21

Sanchez, Jose (c), Amistad 20
Sanchez, Pablo (c), Penalver 35
Sanchez, Jose (c), Villano--
Sanchez, Juan Jose (c), San Rafael 24
Sanchez, Hilario (c), Merced 15
Sandoval, Jose (c), Monte 126
Sagrera, Domingo (c), Jesus del Mone 64
Santana, Francisco (c), Plata 2
Sedeno, Agustin (c), Aguila 109
Silvera, Juan de la C. (c), San Miguel 151
Siguenza, Aniceto (c), Genios 13
Sobrado, Miguel (c), Jesus del Monte--
Soto, Bartolome (c), Genios 4

Tello, Antonio (c), Salud 76
Torres, Luis (c), Monte 299
Torres, Jose (c), Luz 41
Torrens, Jaime (c), Merced 73

Uller, Francisco (c), Obrapia 38

Valdes, Bruno (c), Empedrado 21
Valdes, Juan (c), Compostela 129
Valdes, Ramon (c), Lealtad 25
Valdes, Manuel (c), Sta. Barbara 176
Valdes, Manuel (c), Maloja 17
Valdes, Jose (c), Manrique 55
Valdes, Jose (c), Corral 108
Valdes, Juan (c), Vives 40
Valdes, Esteban (c), San Nicolas 109
Valdes, Lorenzo (c), Salud 65
Valdes, Juan (c), Trocadero 46
Valdes Villamiel, Juan, Empedrado 48
Villega, Manuel (c), Estrella 78
Venate, Jose (zapatero), Jesus del Monte 15
Veranes, Francisco A., Cuba 53
Vega, Ramon de la (c), Angeles 4

Xiques, Felipe (c), Mercaderes 76

FROM *DIRECTORY OF ARTS, COMMERCE, AND INDUSTRY OF HAVANA 1859* (FROM THE BIBLIOTECA MUSEO DE LA HABANA).

Tobacco sellers and brands, Havana, 1859:

Alvarez y Hermanos, Julian, 120 San Nicolas Street: Henry Clay, 1a, Diana, Nalon, Excelsior, Felipa, Flor de Henry Clay, Flor Columbia Britanica, Francisco, Antonio de Granada, Franck Pierce, La Selecta Preferida de Julio Levi.
Alvarez, Marcelino, 7 1/4 Manrique Street: La Luna de Valencia, La Ramoncity.

Alvarez Gonzalez, Manuel, 65 Apodoca Street: El Valor de la Rama, superior valor de la Rama.

Alvarez Cuebas, Francisco, 78 San Ignacio Street and 11 O'Reilly Street: La Divina Fe.

Alvarez, Lazaro, 107 Campanario Street: El Triunfo de Bailen.

Alvarez, Manuel, 11 San Juan Street, 65 Apodoca Street, 116 Escobar Street: Fidelidad.

Alonzo, Valentin, 43 San Juan Street: Flor de Valentin Alonso, Dejalma, Flor de Rio Seco.

Alonzo, Jose, 72 San Juan Street: El Sol de Californias.

Alzamora, Federico, 117 Campanario Street: El Emperador Nicolas, La Luna, La Veneciana, La Jardinera Sevillana.

Alcazar, Miguel de, 51 Ricla Street: Mi Nombre, Levi, La Nacion Espanola, Estandartes y Escarapelas de las Naciones de Europa.

Alegre, Ramon, 96 Lealtad Street: Key Brand, La Amelia, La Estrella del Oeste, Star of the West, La Puerta de Llave.

Alsina y fina, Jose, 95 Campanario Viejo Street: La Manola, JoseFina.

Ala, Ecsequiel, 106 Aguila Street: El Cerrito, Fanny Esler.

Amay Ramon, 9 San Lazaro Street: Un dia de Reyes en la Habana.

Amat, Manuel, 21 San Jose Street: El Boa, El Recinto de Nervion, La Gloria, La Avilesina.

Amores, Manuel, 14 Galeano Street: La Union, M. Amores.

Acevedo y comp, Jose (n.a.): Flor de Pensamiento.

Andreu y Rojas, 117 Reina Street: El San Francisco, El Designio.

Andreu y comp., Jose, 152 Lealtad Street: La Angelita.

Angulo, Gregorio, 87 Aguila Street: J.D.

Alburne, Bernardo, 58 Rayo Street: La Caolb, La Flor de Albuarne.

Aday, Pedro, P., 190 Maloja Street: Las Cuatro Estaciones.

Azpeachea, Maria de la Concepcion, 89 Animas Street: La Sacerdotista, Peruana.

Arau, Felix, 118 calzada del Monte: Minerva, Los Vijilantes, La esquisita de Ricardo, La Opera, Arnau.

Aranda, Jose, 37 San Juan Street: La Rosalia, La Rosa de Georgia, La Regina, El Buen gusto, Trieste.

Aragon, Salvador, 11 Oficios Street: La Reforma Aragonesa, the Listlebet, The Potomag Riber Guits Nacionals.

Armenteros, Lorenzo, 116 San Rafael Street: Los Tres Monos.

Arechavaleta y Zabala, Campanario Street at corner of Los Sitios: La Leonesa, Nueva Albion.

Asay, Celestino, 2 Carmen Street: Florita, Filoteo, Asay, El Humo, Union, Industria Solicitada.

Asay, Isidoro, 10 Trocadero Street: La Ovetense, La Corredoria, La Epoca.

Anes y Solanes, 66 calzada del Monte: El Castillo de Agramont, El Privilegio.

Arango, B. comp., Valentin, 125 Campanario Street: La Cautiva, El Galeote Nobleza.

Arguelles y Hermano, Joaquin, Consolacion Street.

Arrumbado, Jose, 51 San Nicolas Street: Argelina.

Arguelles y Hermano, Joaquin, 8 Cuba Street.

Arguirre y comp., Jose, 73 Rayo Street: Churuca.

Ayala y Maldonado, Jose, 27 1/2 San Juan Street: Knickerboacker Battle Moment, Baltimore club.

Ayla, Jose Maria, 27 1/2 San Juan Street: Triunbirato.

Azperti, Antonio, 68 Consulado Street: La Italia.

Aello, Jose de Orta, 92 Rayo Street: La Olallita.

Barbosa, Jose, 60 Industria Street: La Moneda.

Barbery, Jose, 14 Concordia Street: La Monserrate.

Barcena y comp., 4 Maloja Street: Nelsson, La Llave, El Sena.

Bastarrechea, Leonardo, 64 Merced Street: La U, La Cachucha.

Barrera, Joaquin, 60 Neptuno Street: La Victoria, Carolina, Franklin, Flor de Barrena, J.B., James King of William.

Barrera, Jose de Jesus, 63 Prado: El Regocijo de Barrera y Ruiz.

Barreto, Leoncio, 95 Mercaderes Street, Flor del Fumar.

Bazar, Juan, 69 San Ignacio Street: Las Ninas de J.B.

Bazan, Jose Morales, 184 calzada del Monte: Potencias Beligerantes.

B. May y comp., 6 Obrapia Street: El Profeta.

Bernal, Jose, 331 or 131 Aguila Street: La Costera Habanera.

Benitez y comp., Antonio: Mi Fama el Universo acalma, La Mercantil, Iturbe, Republica Mejicana, Plan de senales de Mazarredo.

Betancourt, Nicolas, 82 Villegas Street: Correo Telegrafico.

Beltran y Garizurieta, Antonio, 148 Escobar Street: Lard Welington, Beltran y Garizurieta, Flor de A. Beltran y Garizuurieta.

Bencoechea, Jose, 88 Rayo Street: La Real.

Bibian de Casas, Erancisco, 133 calzada del Monte: Gicotencal.

Borge, Jose El, 52 calzada del Monte: El Sol, El Sol de Cuba, Aguila de Oro, Justita, La Genovesa, Los Doce Meses, Habana Las Pleyadas.

Botin, Antonio, 28 Reina Street: La Alianza, A.B., Superior Alianza.

Brendes, F., 90 Mercaderes Street: Cavinet, Dona Augusta.

Brito Perfecto, 387 calzada del Monte: El Mono.

Bueno, Jose, 179 and 121 Jesus del Monte and 123 Bernaza Street: El Sol de Veracruz, La Maria Luia, La Crimea, Lugarita, El Bobo de Coria, Chalon, Flor de Jose Bueno.

Bustamente, Carlos, 115 Virtudes Street: Nueva Empresa, Bustamante.

Cabarga y comp., Antonio, 25 Galeano Street: La Abertina, La Coronacion, La Marina, El Maino, El Artillero, Ocristi segars, La Corona, La Sobresaliente, La Infancia, El Marinero. Cabarga, Jose, 129 Cuba: J. de Cabarga y comp., Batalla de Alma.

Cabrera, Antonio, 35 Apodaca Street: El Globo de Godar.

Caballero, Vicente, 156 calzada del Monte: Mi Fama.

Castanedo, Juan Jose, 45 Angeles Street: La Fe, Juan J. Catanedo, Evaristo San Miguel, Diosa de las Antillas, Flor de Castanedo.

Castanon, Francisco J., 14 and 16 Angeles Street: Francisco J. Castanon, General Laborde, Emilia, Castanon, Calesero, General Tacon, bella Emilia.

Castella, Ramon, 14 Escobar Street: Reina Victoria, El Vicio Universal.

Carbajal, Santullano y Comp., 4 Horqueta Street: La Azucena, Los Principados.

Calafell, Juan, 30 calzada del Monte: Diamantes de la Corona.

Castillo y comp., J., 70 Prado: S.N.G., S.N., El Acuerdo, Flor del Acuerdo, Noiega.

Castillo, Nicolas, del, 2 Indio Street: El Cuatro de Marzo.

Carrillo, Jose, 261 calzada del Monte: Tacio.

Castello y comp., 156 Campanario Street: Para Mi, Luisa Miller, El Paseo, Flor del Paseo, Luceros.

Campos Hermanos, in Bejucal: Cuatro Sobrinos, Flor de Campos, Dona Augusta, Dos Amigos.

Caruncho, Antonio, 104 Campanario Street: Intinidad, Super Omnia.

Calahorra, Manuel, 59 Reina Street: Espana.

Calonge, Carlos, in Bejucal: La Eloisa.

Carrero, Jose, 145 Estella Street: Los Hereos de Puebla, La Ilustracion, Plan de Senales de Mazarredo, Abecedario manual con una y dos manos, senas de guarismos para sordos mudos.

Carreras, Antonio, 41 Blanco Street: Dolorita.

Cerda, German de la, 35 Corrales Street: La Sifia, El Veguero Cubano.

Correa, Jose, 62 San Juan Street: Mis Hijas.

Cerda, Anastasio de, 1 Corrales Street: La Aventura.

Corujo y comp., Luis, 158 Neptune Street, 30 Blanco Street and 114 Obrapia Street: Que se yo, Hija del Regimento, El comericante, Flor de Corujo, Missoury.

Cepeda, Jose A., 123 Sitios Street and 192 Lealtad Street: La Valentina, La Esposicion de Londres, Flor de Leando P. Zepeda, superior de tabacos.

Correa Jose, Villavicencio, 50 Figuras Street: Montecristo y Mercedes, Flor de Mi Vega.

Correa, Rufino, 78 Angeles Street: El Jardin de Pedro Correa, Proteccion del Sr. de Puche, hermanos y comp., Deleite de Carmita, Filmore.

Costales, Serafin, 1 Factoria Street: El Libano, La Tutelar, Rio Sacramento, La Flor de Costales, Casimira, Antonio Muro, B. costales, Viriato, La Juventud.

Codina, Jaime, 35 Estrella Street: La Reova, Cinco de Orioin, El Rifle.

Coca e Iglesias, 22 Real de la Salud: Isabel, Amelia.

Cortada, Sebastian, in Santiago de las Vegas: Leon de Oro, Leon, Ninfa.

Coy, Juan , 73 San Ignacio Street: La Mantuna.

Chenar Pablo. F., 47 O'Reilly Street: Los Tres Leones.

Crespo, Bernardino, 231 Corrales and 23 Neptuno Streets: Laberinto, Fragua Pajaro, Mono Vulcano.

Crespo E., 81 Industria Street: Flor de Crespo, F.B.

Crespo, Francisco, 86 Edigo Street: La Perla Jerezana.

Crespo y Carrilo, B., 228 San Nicolas Street: El Pajaro.

Clausen y comp., Enrique Street: Flor del Pacifico, Flor de la Lena.

Clisen, Jose J., 75 Gervasio Street: Esmero, El Fuego, Maria Antonieta, Vuelta del Rio.

Cruz, Miguel de la, 160 San Miguel Street: La Andreita.

Curbelo, Agustina, 111 Maloja Street: El Tamarindo.

Cueto, Jose, 99 Sitios Street, Los Cuatro Hermanos.

Cubrey, 32 Obispo Street: Josefita, Osceola, Cubrey.

Coca, J., 110 Compostela Street, La Meridiana.
Castilla, Manuel, 10 Horqueta Street.

Dehesa, Jose, 70 Ricla Street: La Flor Chinesca.
Delgado, Agustin, 147 San Migel: La Ladi Franklin.
Diaz y comp., Roman, 93 Consulado Street: La Espanola, Distinguida Espanola, La Cosmopolita.
Diaz, Joaquin, 265 calzada del Monte: El Solitario.
Diaz, Joaquin, Devero, 173 Monte: Alejandrowe, El Tropico, Maria Alejandrowe.
Diaz, Benigno, 141 Real Street, Regla: Pruebame y Veras, el Paraiso de Regla.
Diaz, J.F.N., 13 Angeles Street: Correo de J.F.N. Cronis de J.V.D.
Dime, Juan: Guadalupe, Josefita, Flor de Rio Hondo.
Donglos, Gregorio: El Importador.
Duran, Juan: The Gallanfirement.
Duran, Juan, 79 Oficios Street: El Tio Caniyitas.

Esteban, Manuel, 63 Industria Street: El Pendon de Castilla.
Estevill, Juan, 108 San Nicolas Street: El Mayoral.
Escrita, Blas, 16 Campanario Street: El Perfecto.
Estrada, Antonio, 100 Campanario Street.

Fatregas, Jose, 148 Aguila Street: Rigolete, Rodolfo.
Falgueroiles, 28 Horqueta Street: Bayadera.
Fernandez Pellon, Cristobal: La Flor de Caperusa.
Fernandez, Francisco Maria, 146 Real Street, Regla: El Sol de Regla.
Fernandez, Fermin, 72 Compostela Street: Tabla pitagorica, Mendoza.
Fernandez y comp., Valentin, 10 Teniente Rey Street: La Union Universal.
Fernandez y comp., 28 Obrapia Street: La Higuera, La Especial, La Coqueta, La Abeja, Laberinto.
Fernandez Cardin, 132 Industria Street: R. Fernandez Cardin, Fragancia, Pinta, Fernandina.
Fernandez Campo, 54 Consulado Street: El Indio Enamorado.
Fernandez, Jose, 71 Sol Street: Hernan Cortes.
Fernandez y comp., Jose Maria, 5 Figuras Street: El Mundo se admira, Flor de Fernandez, El Orve se admira.
Ferreria y Busta, 81 Industria Street: La Eleccion, el Orve.
Ferran, Francisco: Los dos Leones, Dos Cabanas, Dos Palmas.
Felin, Jose: Fe y Esperanza, Salome.
Fina, Jose A., 11 Concordia Street: Jose Fina, La Manola.
Fontanilles y Miro, 55 Vives Street: Palacio de Cristal.
Folgueras y comp., Jose Maria, 28 Salud Street: Flor de Folgueras, La Rennion.
Fort, Jose, 89 San Ignacio Street: La Constancia, Fidelidad.
Fort, Jose, 67 San Lazaro Street: Sevillana, Flor Sevillana, Reservados, Siempre Viva.
Fontanills, 8 Mercaderes Street: Meridiana.
Fora, George T. de, 64 Horqueta Street: Banana, La Naranja, La Uva.
Frasquieri, Jose, 105 Virtudes Street: Estrella Habanera, Habera, Aurora, Fraquieri, J.F. P. Superior Frasquieri.
Fuster y comp., Gaspar, 103 Jesus Maria Street: Taglioni.
Fuster y comp., C., 1 Teniente Rey Street: La Mallorquina.
F.B., 81 Industria Street: Chuchito.

Garcia, Nicolas, 10 Trocaderos Street: Fir ode Garcia.
Garcia, Jose Jl, 124 Reina Street: Britanica.
Garcia, Jose Antonio, 28 Rayo Street: La Lejitima, Nocotiano, El Telemaco.
Garcia, Cecilio, 217 San Rafael Street: Dos Hermanos.
Garcia, Juan, 9 1/2 Companario Street: Las Ramos de Oro.
Garcia, Jose. 42 Amagura Street: La ingenuidad, La Asturiana.
Garcia, Joaquin, 119 Bernaza Street: La Primera.
Garcia y comp., 11 1/2 Obispo Street: Antonio Garcia y comp., Sultan, Region de Oro.
Garcia, Cecilio, 183 Aguila Street: El Veguerro Enamorado, Soy fiel.
Garcia, Andres, 69 Maloja Street: La Andreita.
Garcia, Valdivieso y comp., 125 Lealtad Street: El Capitolio, La Flor de Arroyave.
Garcia de los Rios, Francisco, 47 San Juan Street: Flor de Rio Seco.
Garcia, Manuel, Empedrado Street: La Liga Europea.
Garcia, Juan, 91 Companario Street: La Rama de Oro.
Garcia, Fulgencio, 56 Aguila Street: El segundo Garcia.
Galvan, Francisco, 111 Maloja Street: Emperatriz, Suspiro.
Gonzalez, Eulogio, 114 Lealtad Street: Mi madre, Ramilete de Aroma, Bellas Artes, Camila, Ventura, Rapidez, Ancla de Oro, Mensajero.
Gonzalez, Andres: La Flor de Londres.
Gonzalez del Real, Pedro, 115 Virtudes Street: Napoleon.
Gonzalez, Jose Hilario, 34 Amistad Street: El Mensajero, La Gracios, La Puertoriquena, Las Graciosas, Islenas.
Gonzalez Pumariega, Jose, 12 Figuras Street: El rio Sella, La Flor de un dia, El Cesar, La Flor de Jose Pumariega.
Gonzalez, Felipe, 183 calzada del Monte: Mi Bullarengue.
Gonzalez, Domingo, 23 Escobar Street: Delicias de Rojas, Delicias.
Goicouria, Carmen, 153 Cuba Street: Hoya de la Mar, Rio Hondo, Consolacion.
Gordon, Manuel, 30 Jesus del Monte: La Reclutadora.
Gomez, Manuel, 27 San Rafael Street: Indio Errante, Dos Hermanas, Patria.
Gomez, Ildefonso, 31 Salud Street: Permanente Pepilla.
Garcia, Jose de Jesus, 124 Reina Street: Georgia.
Granados, Angel, 66 Jesus Maria Street: Carroza de Venus.
Graupera y comp., 71 calzada del Monte: La Lira de Oro.
Guederiaga, Ramon, 3 Obrapia Street: Para V., La Vascongada, Simon Bolivar.
Guerra y Palacio, Loret, 2 San Juan Street: La Catedral.
Gutierrez, Pedro, 138 San Lazaro Street: La Semiramis, Fray Gerundio, Ilustre Duque de la Victoria, Carlota.
Gutierrez, Tomas, 78 calzada del Monte: T. Gutierrez, La Ritoca, Prufohia.
Guanabens, Joaquin, 18 Obispo Street: El General Concha.

Hernandez, D., 32 calzada del Monte: Los dos amigos.
Hernandez, Flores, Luis, 130 Neptuno Street: El Veguero, Capitan, C. Alchorn.
Hernandez, Jose Ildefonso, 8 Angeles Street: Caridad, Leonorcita, Isleta.
Heeno, Jose Bernardo, 5 Angeles and 81 Belascoain Streets: La Simpatia, Jesus Peregrino, La Patente.
Herrera, Jose de, 13 San Rafael Street: Calidad y buen sabor.
Hoz, Manuel de la, 155 Habana Street: Un tirador entisiasta.

Inchaustegui, Felix, 255 calzada del Monte: F.I. y comp.
Incera: Gran Antilla.
Iglesias y comp., Ramon, 22 Salud Street.
Izquierdo, Pedro, 529 calzada del Monte: El Leon de Castilla, el Sol del Horcon.

Jaen y Panadero, 19 Sitios Street: Jaen y Panadera, Mejor.
Jorda, Francisco in San Antonio de los Banos: American, Fortuna, Favorita.
Jimenez, J.R., 136 San Nicolas Street: Diadema, La Rueda.
Jose, Joaquin, 20 Jesus Maria Street: La Confianza.
J.M.A., 91 Galeano Street: Paulina.
J.S.D.,: Robert Peell.
J.D.B., 84 Sol Street: Flor de Belen.
J.D.J., 8 Horqueta Street: El Veguero Cubano.

Lizano y comp., 151 Aguila Street: La Flor de Navarra.
Lopez, Jose Carlos, 49 Refugio Street: Macepa.
Lopez, Felipe, 75 Lagunas Street: La Ceres, La Proserpina.
Lopez y Torres, 142 Calzada del Monte: El Tiempo.
Lopez, Diego, 69 San Ignacio Street: El Delfin.
Loredo, Isidro R., 3 Empedrado Street: La Tortola de las Vegas.
Loredo, Francisco, 109 San Rafael Street: La Alambra, La Palma Celebrada, La Puntualidad Veguera, Rusco de la O.
Llanusa, Juan, 127 Reina Street: Washington.
Lobek, T. The., Monkeis.
Larranaga y comp., 46 San Miguel Street: Por Larranaga, La Guipuscu... Alexander 2., Real Rous.
Landrogue, Ramon, 21 Escobar Street: Guaniguanico, La Perla Cubana, La Mariposa.
Llavina, Jose, 18 Acosta Street: Flor de Habana.
Lluch y Mascaro, 9 Obispo Street: El Gas Villanueva, Congreso.
Lopez y Gonzalez, 38 Estrella Street: La Paz de China, Flor de Lopez y Conzalez, El Prototipo.

Madera y comp., 119 San Rafael Street: J.M. Madera y comp., La Plata.
Machado, Manuel, 28 Salud Street: Hojas de Oro, J.P.M., Palma.
Maso y F., Juan, 61 Estrella Street: Illustre Principado o las Cuatro Letras.
Matas, Cayetano, 12 Sol Street: El Plano de la Machina.
Mata y comp., Antonio, 37 O'Reilly Street: La Torre de Tavira.
March y Blanco, 17 Oficios Street: Contand el Valles.

Moneda la, Jose Barbosa, 69 Industria Street.
Martinez, Rita, 91 Coloma de Galeau: Eterlina.
Martinez, de Aparicio, Felipe, 117 1/2 Concordia: El Regimiento numo. 12.
Martinez y Bor (Ibor), Vicente, 108 Animas Street: El Principe de Gales, Martinez de Bor, Liverpool, La Pistola, La Argelina, Mina Cubana, Martinez.
Martinez, Jose Maria, 2 Carmen Street: El Principe Dfalma.
Martinez y comp., Eugenio, 6 Obispo Street: Algo sabemos, Sobra lugar.
Martinez e hijos, 195 calzada del Monte: Adlaida, Asco, Etelvina.
Mayorga, Manuel, Bernals: La Primera del Orbe, La Vuelta de Abajo.
May, Santiago, R., 68 Animas Street: Usted gusta?
Maza, Benigno, 13 Obispo Street: El Combate, Dios la proteje, Desafio.
Mendoza, Tomas, 51 Estrella Street: Filadelfia.
Mina, Felix, 86 San Rafael Street: Modelo de la Antiguedad.
Misi y Pla: Teresito.
Miranda y comp., Rafael, 75 Sol Street: El Pollito.
Morera, M., Maloja Street: Candita, Caucusana.
Morales, Bazan Jose, 148 calzada del Monte: Hercules.
Morales, Jose, 77 Lealtad Street: La Flor de Morales, La Selina, La Matilde.
Molina, Carlos, Amargura Street: Fama de la Marina Habanera.
Montoro y Santiago, Jose Maria, 71 San Miguel Street: Flor de la rama, La Loteria.
Moleso, M., 86 Cuba Street: Flor de M. Moleso.
Morera hijo, 20 San Miguel Street: Morera.
Moreno, Bartolome, 80 Dragones: La Prensa.
Montoro y hermano, 80 San Rafael Street: La Loteria, La Sultana, Montoro, La Americana, Oregon.
Montero, Rafael Jose, 2 Horqueta Street: La Pilarsito.
Macipe, Bruno, 32 calzada del Monte.
Munoz, Francisco J., 79 San Lazaro Street: La Titis, Gran Cartago.
M.A.N., 80 Dragones Street: Flor del Tropico.

Nansa, Carlos, 20 Santa Clara Street: La Providad, La Duquesa de Medina.
Nora y comp., 22 Reina Street: Superior Globo.
Nunez y Herrera, Luis, 34 Aguacate Street: Fortuna contra Fortuna.

Partagas, Jaime, 1 Cristina Street: Flor de Tabacos de Partagas y comp.
Pando, Jose, 43 Virtudes Street: El Convenio, La Alizanza de Inglaterra y Francia, La Zarzuela.
Parets y Pons, Pablo, Pablo, 91 Reina Street: Jenny Lind, Niagara, Gefferson, El Coloso de Rodas, El Yumuri, El Caminante, Esperanza, realizada, Suenos, G.R.A., Sebastopol, Parets y Pons.
Pastrana, Francisco J., 72 Manrique Street: La Flor Cubana.
Pascual, Jeronimo Garcia, 65 San Lazaro Street: Elvira.
Pesiche, Juan Bautista, 51 Palomar Street: El Ruisenor, El Amor Cubano.
Pelleija, Buenaventura, 59 Oficios Street: Las Tres Flores.
Perez Delgado, Jose Agustin, 105 San Miguel Street: Lady Franklin.
Pellon, Cristobal Fernandez: Flor de Caperusa.
Pozas, Damaso de las, 8 Concordia Street: El Cometa.
Porta, Joaquin, 11 Obispo Street: Mi fama por el orbe vuela.
Pozo e hijo, Nicolas, 62 Obispo Street: El Siglo XIX, La Guarina.
Pozas y Puigdengolas, San Lazaro Street: Flor de la Vuelta de Abajo, Pozas y Puigdengolas.
Plat, Antonio, 218 Manrique Street: La Nina Adelaida.
Pujadas, Francisco, 17 Jesus Maria Street: Las dos Hermanas, Flor de Pujadas.
Pujadas y Llanguer, 67 Antonmoco Street: La Mas bella, La Mariposa, el Mundo al reves, Mundo nuevo, La Mia, Misericordia.
Puente, Santiago, 24 San Miguel Street: La Corunesa, El Capricho de las Bellas Cubanas.
Pumariega, Jose, 12 Figuras Street: Flor de Pumariega, Rio Sella.
Pujol, Antonio, in Santiago: El Tulipan.

Quevedo, Matias, 123 Concordia Street: Anversois, Diablo Marino, Flor del Duende.
Quevedo, Damian, 96 San Miguel Street: La Descubierta, D.G., de Quevedo, Damian, Fontcuberta, de Fontcuberta, D.F.
Quevedo y T., 8 Mercaderes Street and 55 Corrales Street: La Meridiana, La Esposicion.
Quesada y hermano, Antonio, 87 Aguila Street: Va bien.
Quintela, Jose, 185 Gervasio Street: La Jardinera.

Rabago y Gastambide, 10 Zanja Street: Cervantes, Cabllero del Cisne.
Ramirez, B.V., 142 San Miguel: La Gemela, Castano, Luis Napoleon, Ramirez.

Rayon y comp., Manuel, 8 Cuchillo Street: Dos hemisferios, Iberia.
Ramirez, Juan, 183 Jesus del Monte: El Transporte.
Rabell y comp., 162 Industria Street: Gobden Williams, Il Ambrosia, Sabrosa.
Ramirez, 72 Rayo Street: Buena Aroma.
Ramon, Isidro, 21 Mercaderes Street: Una Corona, Tres Coronas.
Rondueles y Menendez, 122 Manrique Street: Rendueles, Habana, La Flor Tropical, La Salud, La Pedrera, La Camagueyana, La Infiesta y Castro, de Riofeo, J.Menendez.
Revilla, Buenaventura G., 82 Gervasio Street: La Mulata.
Reina, Manuel de, 62 Dragones Street: La Granadina, La Caimana, La Chata, La Emilia, Alcazar, La Alhambra, M. Reina.
Rencurrel, Bernardino, 51 Damas Street: Astrea, B.R., Con tinta, Rencurrel.
Rey, Julian, 11 Salud Street: Usted vera.
Rionda, Manuel de la, 133 Animas Street: Legalidad, Flor de la Legalidad, Riera, Oregon, Nada Sabemos, Silistria, Marcia Stuard, Gibraltar, Principe de Argel, Opera, Babilonia, Mascara.
Rionda, Jose A. de la, 159 Reina Street: Francisco de la Rionda y Alvarez, Pensilvania, La mejor de la Habana, Langredo.
Rimon y comp., Francisco, 30 Aguila Street: El Monumento.
Rio, Francisco Perez, 18 Figuras: Flor de Ines, Pruchinela, Rochester, Sevillano, Unica Flor de Rio, Rio de la Plata, Knikerboquer.
Rios, Francisco G., de los, 62 San Juan Street: Flor de Rioseco.
Rivero, Jose Il, 62 San Juan Street: Mis dos hijos, Candelaria.
Ridas, Castillo y comp., 222 1/2 Manrique Street: Figaro, La Flor de Andres Rivas, el Telegrafo Transatlantico.
Rosero, Jose Ines, 53 San Juan Street: Mis dos hijas.
Romay, Pedro, 30 Figuras Street: Los tres primos.
Rojas, Juan de: La Inesita.
Rodriquez Rubio, Ignacio, 69 Villegas Street: Rodriguez, Rubio, el Pabellon Mejicano.
Rodriguez y comp., Juan, 156 Cerro Street: La estrangera, Principe de Asturias.
Rodriguez, Juan, 95 Jesus del Monte: La pira del Amor.
Rodriguez, Jose, 80 Dragones Street: Los Azules de Zabanache.
Rodriguez, Nazrio, 14 Picota Street: La Divina Pastora.
Rodela, Jose, 80 San Lazaro Street: Marta, La Industria Cubana.
Rojas, Andres J.: El Disignio.
Rojo, D., 9 Luz Street: Rojo D.
Rosas, Felix: Lola Montes, Nueva Orleans.
Rosas, Julio: Paquita.
Rosas, Jose, 59 Oficios Street: El Correo.
Romero, Juan B., 6 Obispo: La Estrella fija, Motezuma.
Ronquillo, A., 77 Maloja Street: El Acierto.
Roig y comp., Antonio, 99 Sol Street: La Salvadora, La Agradecida, Reina La Victoria, Vigilancia.
Rocosa y comp., Francisco, 169 Habana Street: El buen sistema.
Romero, Juan Bautista, 110 Cuba Street: Reina de las Antillas.
Rua, Canet y comp., 125 1/2 Animas Street: La Estrangera.
Ruiz Seco, Antonio, 85 Maloja Street: Leviathan, Suizos, Sol Habanero.
Ruiz y Gaitan: Ruiz y Gaitan, La Brisa.
Roig y Gonzalez, 2 Colon Street: Correo Ingles.
Rodriguez, Francisco, 2 Refugio Street: Flor de America.
Ruiz, Unanue y comp., 68 Consulado Street.

Saborin, Juan, 22 Indio Street: Fulton.
Sais y comp., Miguel, 35 Amargura Street: La Araucana, la Fortuna de Navajas.
Sanchez, Manuel, 125 1/2 Animas Street: Corona Ducal.
Sanchez, Narciso, 63 San Lazaro Street: El Deleite Cubano.
Sainz y comp., Mateo, 59 Reina Street: El Ferro-carril, M.G. Espana, el Divan, La Rama de Rio-hondo, el Dorado.
Saldana, Juan Antonio 46 1/2 Reina Street: Manufactor, La Redoma Encanta.
Salazar, Jose Tomas, Compostella Street: La Risita.
San Juan, J., 28 Cuba Street: Los Intrepid Bomberos.
Salat y comp., Antonio, 316 calzada del Monte: Garantizada, Brillante Corintia, Dulce Pina, Superior Dulce Pina.
Sala, Manuel de la, 92 Virtudes Street: ?U--bog, Flor de Sala, San-Slich, La Dignidad, Flor de las Antillas.
Silvestre y Anes, 66 calzada del Monte: Castillo de Agramont.
Somonte, Diego, 118 Vives Street: Principado de Asturias.
Suarez, Francisco, 30 Factoria Street: Gusto del Mono.

Suarez, Francisco, 165 Morrales Street: Competencia, Actividad, Panamena, Urquiza.
Susini, Luis, 91 Ricla Street, 43 Cuba Street, and 6 3/4 Obispo Street: El Balsamo, Capitan, Flor Inesperada, La Guairena, La Honradez, La Mejicana, Mi Fortuna, Mi Pensamiento, Los Nacionales, La Naval, La Ornitologia, La Popular, Topografia Universal, Vijia del Morro, La Venezolana, La Inesperada (cigarettes).

Tarola, Antonio, 34 Estrella Street: El Africano.
Tapias, Jose, 130 San Rafael Street: Un Desengano a tiempo.
Tapia e Illas, 39 Dragones: La Isla de Cuba.
Taleles, Jose Alejo, 10 Reunion Street: Magnolia.
Temes, Jose Caridad, 3 Cuna Street: Firmeza India.
Toro, Jose Maria, San Miguel Street between Galeano and Aguila: Las conferencias.
Torres y Lopez, 142 calzada del Monte: Flor de Torres y Loopez.
Torres y comp., 46 Obispo Street: Daoiz y Velarde.
Torres, Jose Anillo, 11 O'Reilly Street: Hermosa Consuelo.
Tolivar, Francisco, 20 Factoria Street: La Fontica.
Tolme y comp.: Rosehill.
Trueba y Hernandez, Diego, 118 Maloja Street: Torre de Malakoff, Diego Trueba y comp., Tropical, Vescarbal.
Trueba y comp., Carlos, 83 Ricla Street: De Trueba y comp.

Uriarte y comp., 12 Oficios Street: Uriarte Illustrood, Laffayet.
Urbejo y comp., 47 Escobar Street: La Zaragozana, El Pescador.
Upman y comp., 75 San Miguel Street: Upman La Imperial Bandera, La Constelacion, Columbia, El Desvelo de Tello.

Valdes, Juan Gualberto, 37 San Miguel Street: Amistad y Union.
Valdes, Isidoro, 26 Angeles Street: Los Genizaros.
Valdes, Pablo, 109 Escobar Street: La Resoluccion.
Valdes, Jose Pl, 72 Picota Street: El laurel de Apolo, El Afan.
Velazquez, Pl, 68 Cuba Street: La Habana.
Valdes, Jose Ildefonso, 113 Neptuno Street: Lallebe.
Valdes, Maximino, 41 Zanja Street: La Patria, la Flor de Velez.
Valdes Ramirez, Benigno, 142 San Miguel Street: Consuelo.
Valdes y comp., Juana, 50 Lagunas Street: Madre e hijo.
Valdes, Manuel Ciriaco: La Flor del Arte.
Valmusi, Jose, 8 1/2 Oficios Street: Las Cinco Hermanas.
Valera, Jose, 129 Animas Street: Superior J. Maria.
Valera, Miguel, 148 Animas Street: La Guadalupe.
Varela, Jose, 40 Escobar Street: Cecilia Maria, Estoy en Regla, Johum J. Jalhoung.
Vega, Carlos, 37 Galeano Street: Nectar Cubano, Pebete.
Vega, M. de la, 45 and 41 Reina Street, 71 Calzada del Monte, and 23 Estrella streets: La Flor de Vega, Calendario, Esplicacion del juego del Ajedrez, Figurines de Paris, Flor de la Fama, Fama de L. Hijo, Flor de la Reina, Guia de forasteros de la Habana, Lenguaje de las flores, Lista de la Real Loteria, Reina de las flores, La Fama D. L. Hijo, Non plus ultra, La Fama, el Escojedor, el Rio.
Velez, Juan, 52 Dragones Street: Almirante Colon, La Corina.
Velasco, Torcuato, 2 Carmen Street: Artemisa, Palmeta, Flor de Torcuato Velazco, La Nacioinal, T.M. Enrique.
Vidal y Rivas, Rafael, 28 San Juan Street: El Triunfo de la paz.
Vilaro y D., Juan, 13 Angeles Street: Coronis, La Fortuna de M. V. y D., Lucia de Lammermoor, Esculapio, Eureca, lo hemos encontrado, T.V.
Villamil, Pedro: Tirabeque.
Villaverde, Santos, 66 Amargura Street: Roza de la Habana, La Hija de Villaveerde, Buena Vista.
Villavicencio, Jose, 52 Figuras Street: La Flor de mi Vega, Montecristo y Mercedes.
Va Bien, Joaquin Antonio Quesada y hermano, 87 Aguila Street.

Zahonet, Domingo: Los Recuerdos.

Almanque Mercantil Para 1873, H. E. Heinen, Havana, 1873.

Names of Factories and Brands:

Acosta, Facundo, Bejucal: Cleopatra, Coralina, Facundo, Maravilla, Palmito, Tres Gracias.
Aja y Gomez, Bomba 23: El Misterio

Alonzo, Valentin, Tenerife 47: Alonso Fernandez, Flor de Mi gusto, Flor de Rio Seco, Flor de Valentin Alonso, Mis dos Hijas, Whitman.
Alvarez, Casimiro, Santiago de las Vegas: Celeste Imperio, Flor de Casimiro Alvarez.
Alvarez, Julian, San Nicolas 128: Flor de Franc(isc)o. P. Alvarez, Flor de Julian Alvarez, Francisco A. de Grande, Henry Clay, Primera Diana, Selecta.
Allones, Antonio, Gervasio 27: Confederacion, Confederacion Suiza, Guarina, Isolina, Republica Argentina, Republica de Chile, Republica Peruana, Rey del Mundo, Uruguay.
Alvarez Myano, Manuel, Bejucal: Clay, Calhoun & Webster, Nueva Empresa, Recreo.
Amat, Manuel, Lealtad 110: Avilesina, Boa, Gloria, Recinto de Nervion.
Andrade Ponce de Leon, Francisco, no address: Marino.
Arango, Valentin, Factoria 20: Caliope, Cautiva, El Corsario, Flor de Solon, Flor de Valentin Arango, Stars & Stripes.
Arrigunaga, Fernando, Sol 110: Flor de Arrigunaga, Flor del Arte, Jockey Club, Monte-Cristo.
Alonso, Valentin, no address: Asturica, Banana, Filoteo, Flor de Asay,Flor de Torcuato y Velasco, Florete, Habana, Humo, Industria, Mango, Naranjo, Palmeta, Solicitada, Veguera, Uva.
Allones, Ramon, Animas 131: Flor Extrafina, Margarita de German Canosa, Margarita de Justo Senande, Silfide Argentina, Silfide Chilena, Silfide Oriental, Silfide Peruana.

Bejar y Alvarez, Lealtad 142: Ultramarina.
Bock y Ca., Virtudes 96: A. Bacallao y Ca., Aguila de Oro, Estrella de Chile, Fausto, Flora Apiciana, Flor del Socorro, Freya, La Predilecta, Monopolio, Moscovita, Perla del Pacifico, Principe de Orange, Raleigh, Royal Engineers, Spirit of The Tamer.
Barcenas, Ramon de las, O'Reilly 7: Consecuente, Churruca, Flor de la Moda, Flor de Ricardo y Llera, High Life, Lord Nelson, Manco de Lepanto, Popular, Rectitud, Sena.
Baruete, Leoncio, Mercaderes 6: Flor del Fumar.
Bastarrechea, L, no address: Cachucha, Flor de Bastarrechea, Vega del Jaguey.
Beci y Hermanos, Manuel, San Ignacio 94: Antonica, Columna de Ambos Mundos, Ermita, Rey de Wurtemberg.
Bello, G.A.E., no address: Flor de Socorro.
Builla, Ceferino, no address: Ambarina.
Bedoya y Rodriguez, Aguila & Estrella: Ilustreduque de la Victoria, Semiramis.

Cabarga y Ca., A., Galiano 93: Albertina, Cabarga y Lopez, Corona, Jose Domingo, La Magdalena.
Cabarga, viuda e hijos de J. de, Concordia 103 & 105: Flor de los Tabaco Habanos, Jose de Cabarga y Ca.
Cabrera, Victoriano A., Tenerife 37 & 39: Buen Gusto, Feliz Habana, Flor de la Habana, Flor de Llavina, Flor de Salazar, Imperial, Laureles de la India, Mariscal, Regina, Rosa de Georgia, Rosalia, Serafina, Trieste, Verdi.
Carvajal, Leopoldo, Calzada del Monte 320: Camelia del Japon, Carvajal y Carvajal, Dos Carrajales, Horcon, L. Carvajal, Pena la Deva.
Caruncho, Antonio, Galiano & Zanja 127: Intimidad, Marques de Caxia, Super Omnia.
Castillo y Suarez, Jose, Manrique 226: Aguila Francesa, Figaro, Noriega, Primor Habanero, Pruebese, Rosa Habanera, Voz de la Inteligencia.
Clarens y Ca., Pedro, Escobar 58: El Buen Tono.
Clisen, Jose J., no address: Esmero, Fuego, Jorry Fritz, Maria Antonieta, Vuelta al Rio.
Codina, Jaime, Estrella 19: Cinto de Orion, El Ramillete Habanero, Flor de Codina, Lirio, Redowa, Rifle.
Conill, Juan, Bejucal: Flor de las Vegas, Juan Conill.
Cordier, Isidro, Pinar del Rio: Ancla de Rio-Hondo.
Corujo, Luis, Zanja 96: Camarioca, Comerciante, Flor de Corujo, Flor de C. y Ruiz, Flor del Pais, Hija del Regimiento, Punch, Sin Par.
Costales, Bernardo, Santiago de las Vegas: Clavel de Santiago, Flor de Mayo, Flor de Recio y Costales, Libano.
Crespo, B., Calzadadel Monte 168: Neptuno.
Cueto y Hermano, Luis, Dragones 64: La Granadina.
Chinchurreta y Duarte, Animas --: Aralar, Cabinet, Chincurreta y

Durarte, Diogenes, Flor de Duarte y Ca., Flor de Manrico, Juan de Chinchurreta, Para la Grandeza, ?Que se yo?, Resalaa.

Diaz, Bances y Ca., Estrella 171 & 173: Almirante deRuyter, A No. 1, Bellamar, Carolina, Flor de Diaz, Bances yCa., Flor de P. Bances, Flor de Tomas Diaz, General Mc.Clellan, Mariscal Villars, Old Abe, Paila del Naranjo, Princesa Dagmar, Rochuvar, Un grano fui, Unser Fritz.
Diaz y Diaz, Juan, Salud 17: Para la Aristocracia, Noblesse oblige.
Diaz, Luis, Santiago de las Vegas: Arabella, Chile, Flor de Luis Diaz, Florida, Modelo de la Antiguedad.
Diaz, P., Egido: La Numancia.

Fernandez Alvarez y Ca., Manuel, Santiago de las Vegas: Diego Lopez y Trujillo, Flor Chinesca, Flor de Gomez, Flor de Santiago, Julia, Mina de Oro, Turca, Winfield Scott.
Fernandez Tunon, Francisco, O'Reilly 53: Constancia,Pajaro del Oceano, Torre de Tavira.
Ferran y Dalmantes, F., Reina 60: Dos Cabanas.
Ferreria y Hermanos, Animas 135: Chuchita, Eleccion, Orbe.
Fortun y Ho., Gabriel M., O'Reilly 54: La Vega del Sol.
Fos y Ca., V, Pinar del Rio: Catalana, Eldorado, Emperatriz Carlota, Ultramar.
Furnes y Dorado, Acosta 42: Rio Janeiro.

Galvan, J, Campanario & Estrella: Bella Emperatriz, Emperatriz Eujenia, Firmeza, Oceola, Suavidad, Tamarindo.
Garcia, Jose Antonio, Rayo 28: Flor de J.A. Garcia,Gobernador Stanley, Great Eastern, Iberia, Ingenuidad, J.A. Garcia, Legitima Ambrosia, Legitima de Garcia, Nicotiana, Ponton, Raquel, Rosa de California, Telemaco.
Garcia,Manuel, Santiago de las Vegas: Consuelo, Flor de Manuel Garcia,Iscandro, Luisita, Rivera, Triguenita.
Garcia y Maza, Obispo 25: Andrew Johnson, Rubi, Sultan.
Gonzalez del Valle, Ansselmo, Dragones 4 & 6: Hija de Cabanas y Carbajal.
Gonzalez,Eulogio, Estrella 35: Ella, Ernst Merck,Garibaldi, Incognita, La Africana, Lo mas sublime, Mi Madre, Mi Suegra, Mozart, Pretension, Ramillete de Aromas, Rapidez.
Gonzalez, J.H., Amistad 40: Aguila de Diamante, Central Park,Curiosidad, Dos Sofias, Florida Blanca, Mensagero, Scotch Fusilier Guards.
Gener, Jose, Calzada del Monte 1: Cruz de Malta, El Imperio Aleman, Escepcion, Gladstone, Gloria de Inglaterra, Monopolizacion, Vuelta-Abajo.
Guillo, Eduardo, Oficios 23: Para Usted, Teresita Carreno.
Gutierrez, Francisco, Acosta & San Ignacio: Flor de Francisco Gutierrez.

Larranaga y Ca., San Miguel 58: Alexander II, Guipuzcoana, Por Larranaga, Ready & Rough.
Lopez, ----, Esperanza 5: Esmero de Arroyave, Esquisitos, Flor Agricola, Flor de Fjo, Flor de Mata y Garcia, Flor de Torres y Lopoez, Joven America, Little Mac, Phil Sheridan, Rialto, Sirena, Soberano, Tiempo.
Lopez, Antonio, Neptuno 159: Flor de Antonio Lopez y Ca., Paz de China, Prototipo, Rosa del Valle, Sublime de A. Lopez.

Manrara y Ca., San Pedro 24: El Principe de Gales.
Madrazo, Manuel, Angeles 12: Aceptacion, Europa, Flor de M. Madrazo, Gitanan, Por Madrazo, Reforma.
Marinas, Manuel, Concordia 25 1/2: Flor de Bengocchea, Flor de Marinas, Guillermo Tell, Incomparable, Inmejorable, Judith, La Victoria, Manuel Marinas, Montanesa, Perla del Tabaco, Primavera, Ramona, Real, Reina de la Habana, Tino.
Marrero, Manuel, Bejucal: Aroma del Balsamo, Balsamo y Aroma, Black Warrior, Conchita, Flor del Veguero, Gran Cruz, La Veguera, Palmeta, Para los Aficionados.
Mato, Pedro, Santiago de las Vegas: Aclaracion, Dos Hermanos, General Grant, Penon, Purez de Mato, Sol de Santiago, Venturina, Visitadora.
Menendez y Suarez, Manrique 118: Boschetti, camagileyana, Conde de Bismark, Flor de Rendueles y Menendez, Flor el Todo, Flor Tropical, Infiesta y Castro, Inocencia, J. Menedez, Orden, Pedrera, Rio Feo.
Mestre, A.B., Virtudes 96: Elvira, Estrella de Chile, Flor de M. Valles.

Miranda y Muniz, Escobar 172: La Occidental.
Morales, Jose, Campanario 88: AGuila de Rusia, Celina, Flor de Canela, Flor de J. Venanacio,Flor de Morales, Lord Rivers, Matilde, Meyerbeer, Pelicano.
Morales,M.A., San Rafael 103: Encanto de Cuba, Flor de J. ares, Flor de J.M.M., Realidad.
Murias y Ca., Antonio, Zanja 1: Flor del Mazo, Flor de Murias.
Murias y Ca., Pedro, Corrales 53: Balmoral, Beauregard, Flor de los campos de Cuba, General Lee, Inflecsible, Jackson Calicanto, Meridiana, Palacio de Cristal, Reserva, Walter Scott.

Noriega, Ambrosio, Suarez 87: Ambrosio Moriega, Flor de A. Mata.

Obeso y Cueto, Oficios 21: La flor de Naves.
Obeso y Hermano, Maloja 70: Flor de Alonso Menendez, Flor de la Clementina, Flor de Guerrabella.
Oceguera, Fernando, Zanja --: Flor de Hamburgo, Modestia, Morito, Victoria.
Oceguera, Pablo, San Rafael 70: Flor de P. Oceguera, Voz de Cuba.
Olmo, Ignacio, Angeles --: Brother Jonathan, Comercio, Flora Cubanan, Jojas de Oro, Nueva Albion.

Pando y Ca.,J., Lealtad 129: Acuerdo, Alba, Caoba, Centinela del Rhin, Crema, Danubio, Dulzura, Fina, Flor de Albuerne, Flor de Campo Largo, Lira de Oro.
Parets y Ca., Salvador, San Nicolas --: Army & Navy Club, Broderick, Caminante, Coloso de Rodas, Cometa, Cotorra, Creacion, Esperanza Realizada, Jardin, Jenny Lind, Magnifica, Parets y Pons, Perro, Postres, Rhin, Ritilla, Sancho Panza, Sebastopol, Tomeguin, Yumuri.
Partagas, Jaime, Industria 160: Balsamica, Clemencia, Flor de Tabacos.
Perez del Rio, Francisco, Figuras 32: Flossom de Tabacos, Bouquet de Tobacos, Flor de Ines, Flor del Sevillano, Flor de Tabacos de Gusto, Flor Escepcional, General Prim, Harmonie Club, Legitimidad, Para V. y sus amigos, Rio de la Plata, Sevillano, Tabacos de Gala, Unica Flor de Rio.
Perez y Ca., Jose, Estrella 124: La Sociedad.
Perez y Velez, Manrique 138: El Brillante.
Pinera, Rosendo, Zanja 70: Afan, Felipilla, Flor de Udo, J. Pablo Valdes, La Paulita, Resolucion.
Presmanes y Sobrino, Gervasio 17: Araucana, Flor de Presmanes y Sobrino, Fortuna de Navajas.
Pumariega, J.G., Neptuno 178: Cesar, Flor de Jose G. Pumariega, Flor de Un dia, General Moltke, Incognito, J.G.P., Palo Alto, Reformador, Rio Sella, Sublime de Pumariega.

Reyes y Gonzalez, Anastasio, Bejucal: El Ancla de Oro.
Rico, Manuel, Santiago de las Vegas: Benigno Rico, Habanos, Lima, Luna, Luna llena, Manuel Rico, Media Luna.
Rodriguez, Andres, Dragones 39: Amadeo I Rey de Espana, Earl of Dummore,Flor de S. Juan y Martinez, Granadier Guards, Islenita Cubana, Oliver Jivist, Tica de Bolton.
Rodriguez, Arias y Ca., Carmen 2: Almendaares, Elba, Felicidad de R. Rodriguez, Flor de R. Rodriguez, La Plata, Ocasion, Puente de Agua Dulce, Relamapago, Rico Habano, Union Universal.
Rodriguez y Fernandez, Acosta 42: Flor de Rodriguez y Fernandez.
Rodriguez, Jose Antonio, Jesus Maria 70 & 72: Coloso, El Encanto, Estrella Eija, Gota de Agua, La Infancia, Moctezuma, Nuevo Paraiso, Reina de las Antillas.
Roger y Ca., Pedro, Santiago de las Vegas: Pamo, Rosa de Santiago.
Romay, Julian, Figuras 44: Adela, Cisne, Copetencia de Romay, Flor de Romay, Ria de Vigo, Rudesinda, Tres Primos.
Romero, Juan B., Consulado 91: Cosmopolita, Espanola, Filantropa, Occidental.

Sala, Manuel de la, Virtudes 127: Balsamo, Bayamo, Buen Aroma, Dignidad, Eclectic, Engna Bobos, Extra Malisima, Extra Superior, Flor de las Antillas, Flor Inesperada, Flor de lo Malo, Flor de Sala, Guillermo II, Infra Omnia, Limena, Malisima, Mijicana, Nada hay peor, No me olvides, Our St. John, Pioneer, Si me compras te divertes, Venenosa, Venezolana.
Solar, Francisco G., Jesus Maria 14: Beatriz, Flor de Soalr, Risita.

Temes, Jose C., Ricla 3: Bella Union, Firmeza, India, Pocahontas.

Toloso, Berange y Compa., San Nicolas 152: La Colonial.
Trueba, Diego, Angeles 16: Artesanos, Belencita, Bella de SanLuis, Cometa Viela, Diego Trueba, Dolce Farniente, Sol Habanero, Suizos, Torre de Malakoff, Ultimatum, Vicalbaro.
Tuero,--, Lealtad 102: Australia, Comercial, Flor de Creta, Flor de Ramon Rosales y Ca., Flor de Tuero y Rosales, Indio, Ninfas del Parque, Ristori, Traviata.

Unanue y Hermanos, Consulado 76: Arroyo Hondo, Flor del Valle, Irurac-Bat., Lealtad, Nelson, Pinar del Rio, Por Unanue, Rio San Joaquin.
Upmann y Ca., H., Cuba 64: Constelacion, Flor de la Lena, Flor del Pacifico, Francia, H. Upmann, Japon, Limpia Bandera, Mil Hermosa.

Valle, Suarez y Ca., Virtudes 97: American Jocky Club, El Pebete, La flor de Cuba, Nectar Cubano, Superior de Cuba.
Viejo, Vicente, Companario --:Ballena, Flor de S. Lopez, Ilustre Jovellanos, Integridad, La Grange, Gladstone.
Vidal, Paulino G., Maloja 12: Aurora, Bustamante,D. Pelayo, Florentina, Lealtad Espanola, Napoleon III, Nueva Empresa, Perfeccion, Pretension, San Roman.
Vinas y Ca., J., Bejucal: Antorcha,Campos de Cuba, Corina, Cosecha de 1863, Flor de Aroma, Fundada Esperanza, Habana Industrial, Idea, Mina, Nuevo Mundo, Quinta Escencia, Venturina.
Villar y Villar, Alejandro, Animas 102: A. de Villar y Villar, Flor de Villar y Villlar, Jorge Juan, Pick Pock Club, Viriato,

Zeller, Amando, Tenerife 44: Anzuclo, Boabdil, Boceacu, Columnas de Ambos Mundos, Fiel, Flor de Amando, Inconstancia, Pilotos, Recuerdo, Tancredo, Zuavo.
Zumalacarregni y Ca., Juan M., Oficios 22, plaza de S. Francisco: Buenos Aires, Fatimita, Flor de Zumalacarregui, Introduccion, La Israelita, Modelo, Palmire, Vascongado.

Almancenistas de tobaco en rama.
Tobacco warehouses:

Alemany y Gutierrez, Virtudes 86.
Arguelles y Ca., Ramon, Calzada del Monte 46.

Baringas, Jose, Calzada del Monte 129.
Bartumeu, Estanislao, Calzada del Monte, 125.
Bedoya y Rodriguez, Aguila, 122.
Bengocchea, Jose, San Miguel 54.

Calarza y Ca., Galiano 98.
Canales, Gregorio, Angeles 16.
Carrera y Garcia, Antonio, Calzada del Monte 197.
Casal, Jose del, Calzada del Monte 38.
Castineiro y Sobrino, Calzada del Monte 60.
Cernuda, Joaquin, Calzada del Monte 130.
Codina, Jaime, Estrella 19.
Conill, Juan, Teniente Rey 35.

Diaz, Joaquin S., Calzada del Monte 134.
Dosol, Martin, Neptuno 143.

Elguera, Manuel, Calzada del Monte 106.

Fernandez, Antonio, Calzada del Monte 121.
Fontanills y Gonzalez, Calzada del Monte 133.
Font, Luis, Calzada del Monte 26.
Franchi, Juan Bta., Anton Recio 14.

Garcia Baldes, Nicolas, Trocadero 12.
Gener y Ho., Aguila 130.
Gonzalez, Antonio, Rayo 66.
Gonzalez y Ho., Jose, Calzada del Monte 116.
Gorordo, Hermanos y Ca., Cuba 67.
Gutierrez, Tomas, Calzada del Monte 114.
Gutierez y Hermano, Calzada del Monte 101.

Ibarrondo, Ramon, Cristo 33.

Jane, Miguel, Industria 174.

Llabina, Jose, Acosta 29.
Llano y Helguera, Calzada del Monte 106.
Lopez, Pedro y Antonio, Esperanza 5.
Lueje, Manuel, Calzada del Monte 191.

Martinez, Antonio, Calzada del Monte 50.
Martinez y Ca., Calzada del Monte 183.
Martinez y Hermano, Calzada del Monte 72.
Muniz, Lopez y Ca., Calzada del Monte 223.
Miranda y Ca., Calzada del Monte 50.

Obeso y Hermano, Calzada del Monte 36.
Oteiza, Jose Antonio, Calzada del Monte 22.

Palacio, Gregorio, Riela 98.
Partagas, Jose, Industria 158.
Perez del Rio, Francisco, Figuras 32.
Perez, Hermanos y Ca., Calzada del Monte 105.
Perez, Jose, Calzada del Monte 203.
Perez,Jacinto, Calzada del Monte 115.
Puente, Julian de la, Calzada del Monte 28.

Quevedo y Ca., Calzada del Monte, 167.
Quintana, Fernando, Factoria 1.

Richtering, Guillermo, Trocadero 22.
Rionada y Barcenas, Calzada del Monte 32.
Ravasa, Sebastian, Calzada del Monte 164.
Roig, Juan, Calzada del Monte 172.

S. Julian y Ca., Francisco, Calzada del Monte 20.
Scharfenberg, Kohy y Ca., Calzada del Monte 57.
Suarez, Blas, Calzada del Monte 171.
Suarez y Ca., Genaro, Calzada del Monte, 139.
Suarez y Ho., Joaquin, Calzada del Monte 211.

Tabares y Bustamante, Calzada del Monte 199.
Torrecilla, Luis, Calzada del Monte 111.
Torre, Joaquin de la, Calzada del Monte 74.
Troncoso, Driano, Calzada del Monte 136.

Vinals, Francisco, Bernaza 32.

Zarza, Benito, San Rafael 52.

LIST OF THE "INDEPENDENT " HAVANA CIGAR FACTORIES FROM *HAVANA CIGARS*, COMPILED BY WILLIAM GILL, HAVANA, 1910 (1921).

Owner's Name, Address, House Brand, Year Established (where provided).

Antonia Lopez, Belascoain 2b: Por Larranaga, 1834.
Manuel Lopez, Ray 28: Punch, 1840.
Cifuentes, Fernandez & Co., Industria 172-174, Partagas, 1843.
H. Upmann & Co., Carlos III 159: H. Upmann, 1844.
Sucesores de Juan Lopez, Dragones 6-8: Flor de T. Gutierrez, 1846.
Vales & Co., Galiano 98: R. Allones & Cruz Roja, 1846.
Diaz Bros. & Co., Zulueta 44: El Rey del Mundo, 1848.
R. Garcia Marques, Estrella 19: High Life, 1848.
Segundo Alvarez & Co., Lealtad 110: Flor el Todo, 1855.
Jose del Real, Escobar 170: Filoteo, 1858.
J.F. Berndes & Co., Cuba 64: El Mapa Mundi, 1864.
Vda. de Jose Gener, P. Alfonso 7: La Escepcion, 1867.
Calixo Lopez & Co., Zulueta 48-50: El Eden, 1868.
Nicolas Roig & Co., Rayo 63: El Ecuador, 1870.
Rodriguez, Arguelles & Co., Belascoain 2a: Romeo & Julieta, 1875.
Fernandez, Garcia & Co., Neptuno 170: Flor de A. Fernandez Garcia, 1876.

Antonio Villaamil, Suarez 7: Flor de Puro Habana, 1878.
Diaz & Valdes, Maloja 31: La Miel, 1879.
Manuel Rodriguez, Manrique 188: La Sirena, 1879.
Moreda & Co., San Miguel 85: La Diligencia, 1880.
J.F. Rocha & Co., San Miguel 100: El Crepusculo, 1882.
F. Rodriguez & Co., Galiano 127: Flor de p.A. Estanillo, 1882.
Manuel Campos, Dragones 110: La Devesa, 1882.
Posada & Lopez, Tenerife 57: Aroma de Cuba, 1887.
Behrens & Co., Consulado 91-93: Sol & Luis Marx, 1890.
F.E. Fonseca, Gervasio 128: Fonseca, 1891.
Jose J. Diaz, Someruelos 8: La Convencion, 1901.
F. Garcia & Bro., Reina 30: F. Garcia Hnos, 1902.
Redencion (S.A.), San Miguel 108: Redencion, 1903.
Antonio Allones & Co., Carlos III 225: El Modelo de Cuba, 1904.
The Castaneda C. Factories, Ltd., Virtudes 129: Castaneda, 1904.
C.E. Beck & Co., Figuras & Lealtad: Beck, 1906.
Fernandez,Medina & Co., Gervasio 180: El Ambar, 1907.
Benito Suarez, Reina 137: Flor de B. Suarez.
Morris & Morris, San Miguel 100: La Legitimidad.
Vda de Camach & Son, Santa Clara 7: La Competidora Gaditana.
J. Alvarez & Co., Estrella 100: Flor de Alvarez.
Juan Chao, Estrella 171: La Capitana.
Saavedra & Bro., Marquez Gonzalez 10: Antilla Cubana.
Anselmo Azcano, Carmen 2: La Imposicion.
Maximo Alvarez, San Miguel 113: La Elecion.
Jose Vejar, Maloja 155: Flor de Bejar.
R. Digon, Monte 41: La Rica Hoja.
C.O. Murias, Estrella 25: La Ciudad.
Jose Otero, San Rafael 93: Flor de Otero.
Perez & Bro, Factoria 49: La Sabrosa.
Pedro Sanchez, Paula: La Chiquita.
Rodriguez & Bro, Belascoain 88: El Credito.
Raimundo Hinojosa, Monte 425: La Aroma Tropical.
Jose Diaz y Rodriguez, Someruelos 8: La Oriental.
Meilan & Pita, Manrique 222: La Paz de America.
Francisco Rodriguez, San Ignacio 11: La Union Commercial.
E. Garcia & Sons, Monte 36: La Melodia.
H. Gonzales & Co., Neptuno 153: La Higuera.
J. Ramirez Perez, Fernandina 65: La Conformidad.
Juan M. Bravo, Suarez 2: Flor de J. M. Bravo.
Ramon Cerezo, San Nicolas 266: Flor de Cerezo.
A. Perez Pazos, Esperanza 3: Flor de A. Pazos.
E. Dorado & Co., Estrella 171: El Rico Habana.
Jose Rodriguez, Estrella 121: El Canal.
J.A. Vilalta, Consulado 69: El Fronton.
Benjamin Fuentes, Corrales 131: B. Fuentes.
Arsenio Perez, Belascoain 54: Arsenio Perez.
Angel V. Palacio, Marquez Gonzalez 48: Palacio.
S. Garcia Veiga, Sitios 11: S.G. Veiga.
Florentin Mantill, Marquez Gonzalez 12: El Rey del Mundo.
Vicente Arizaga, Tenerife 31: El Gremio y La Lealtad.
Joaquin Espinosa, Salud 85: La Verdad.
Sinforiano S. en C. Gonzalez, Monte 318 & 320: La Mia.

DIRECTORY OF CIGAR MANUFACTURERS FROM *LEXICO TABACLERO CUBANO* BY JOSE E. PERDOMO HAVANA, 1940.

Name of Firm, Address (Havana unless otherwise noted) and Brand Names.

Fernandez, Palacio y Cia, Maximo Gomez (Monte) 51: Belinda, El Vinyet, Flor de Fernandez Garcia, Gener, Cioconda, Gladstone, Habanos, Hoyo de Monterrey, La Emperatriz de la India, La Escepcion, La Gloria de Inglaterra, La Iberina, La Sin Par, Las Perlas, Palicio, Punch, Santa Felipa, Smart Set, Vuelta Abajo.

Martinez y Cia., Calle Real 200, Marianao: Antilla Cubana, C.E. Bec y Cia., Fine, Flor de Miramar, Frank Halls, King of Havana, La Devesa de Murias, La Feriada, La Flora de Dascall, La Flor de PedroMiro y Cia., La Flor de Zaro, La Imperiosa, La Ranesa, Los Statos de Luxe, Mapa Mundi, Ricoro, Santa Rosaliia, Sol, Troya.

Por Larranaga, Carlos III 713: El Torcillo, Flor de Cimiente, Flor de Zavo, Habanos 1834, La Atlanta, La Flor de Alvarez, La Gloria, La Legitimidad, Petronio, Por Larranaga.

Calixto Lopez y Cia., Agramonte 702: Calixto Lopez, Eden, Flor de Lopez Hermanos, Francisco C. Bances, Lo Mejor, Lopez Hermanos, Los Reyes de Espana, Morro Castle.

Menendez, Garcia y Cia. Ltda., Virtudes 609: El Patio, H. Upmann, Monte Cristo , Particulares.

Rey del Mundo Cigar Company, Padre Varela 852: Casamonte, Cuesta-Rey, Don Candido, Don Ricardo, El Collado, El Uruguay, Fausto, Flor de Allones, Flor de Marques,Flor de Milamores, Flor de Rafael Gonzalez, Fragus de Cuba, La Confederacion Suiza, La Seductiva, La Solera, Rey del Mundo, Sancho Panza, San Sebastian.

Romeo y Julieta, Padre Varela 152: Don Pepin, Falman, Flor de Rodriguez, Arguelles y Cia., His Majesty, La Mar, Maria Guerrero, Romeo y Julieta.

Castaneda-Montero-Fonseca, Galiano 466: Castaneda, El Genio, Filoteo, Fonseca, Hamlet, J. Montero y Cia., Lurline, Para Mi, Real Carmen, Rotario.

Fabrica de Tabacos F. Solaun S.A., Figuras 106: Baire, Boccacio, Figaro, Flor de Solaun, La Nacional.

Cifuentes, Pego y Cia., Industria 520: Caruncho, Cifuentes, Corojo, El Camio Real, El Marques de Caxias, Flor de Alma, Flor de Caruncho, Flor de F. Pego Pita, Flor de P. Rabell, Flor de Tabacos, Flor de Tabacos de Partagas y Cia., Cayarre, La Eminencia, La Flor de J.A. Bances, la Inmejorable, La Insuperable, La Intimidad, La Lealtad, La Tropical, Marques de Rabell, Mi Necha, Modelo de Cuba, Nada Mas, Osceola, Partagas, Partagas & Co., Partagas y Campania, Prudencio Rabell, Rallones, Ramon Allones.

Zamora y Guerra, Maximo Gomez (Monte) 810: Belanza, Coranto, La Flor de Santa Gertuda, La Loma, La Noble Habana, Landsdown, La Zona, Lions, Saint Luis Rey.

Eduardo Suarez Murias y Cia., Luz 3, Arroyo Naranjo: La Radiant, Reva.

Manuel Fernandez Argudin, Norte 25, Marianao: Argudin, Eslava, La Cordialidad, Macabeus, Manuel Fernandez.

J.F. Roch y Cia., San Miguel 364: Bolivar, Flor de Ambrosio, El Crpusculo, La Gloria Cubana, La Glorieta Cubana, La Navarra, La Petenera, Nene.

Tabacalera Cubana, Agramone 106: A. de Villar y Villar, Antonio y Cleopatra, Arlington, Balmoral, Bock & co., Cayos de San Felipe, Clara Maria, Cortina Mora, Cuba, Cubanola, Delmonico's, Don Quijote de laMancha, Dos Cabanas, El Aguila de Oro, El Aguila Imperial, El Fenix, El Pueblo, El Siboney, Estella, Eureka, Flor de Cortina, Flor de F. de P. Alvarez, Flor de Garcia, Flor de Gumersindo, Flor de J.S. Murias y Cia., Flor de M. Lopez y Cia., Flor de Monte Carlo, Flor de Pedro Roger, Flor de Segundo Alvarez,General R.E. Lee, Habana Club, Hamilton Club, H. de Cabanas y Carbajal, Jose Domingo, Joya de San Luis, Justicia al Merito, Katherine & Petruchio, La Africana, La Alhambra, La Antiguedad, La Aristocratica, La California, La Capitana, La Carolina, La Comercial, La Corona, La Coronilla, La Crema de Cuba, La Espanola, La Flor de A. Lopez, La Flor de Cuba, La Flor de Henry Clay, La Flor de Juan Chao, La Flor de Murias, La Flor de Naves, Lqa Flor de Ynclan, La Indiferencia, La Meridiana, La Opulencia, La Pazde China,La Perfeccion, La Perla de Cuba, La Princesa de Gales, La Prominente, La Prosperidad, La Reina del Oriente, La Reserva, La Rosa Aromatica, La Rosa de Santiago, La Savoie, La Selecta, La Tosca, La Traviata, La Vencedora, La ventana, La Virtud, L. Carbajal, Lojcoln, Lords of England, Manuel Garcia Alonso, Manuel Lopez y Cia., Pedro Murias y Ca., Privilegio, Puck, Santa Damiana, Shakespeare, The Derby, Victor Hugo, Waldorf, Waldorf Astoria, Walter Scott.

The Fernandez-Havana Cigar Co., Marti 64, Guanabacoa: Amor de Cuba, Casco de Oro, Don Alfonso, El Bataclan, Flor del Todo, Jose Jimenez Perez, La Bonita, La Democracia, Lord Beaconsfield, Mascota.

Jose L. Piedra, Reina 404: Jose L. Piedra, Ovalo Rojo, Piedra.

Lobeto y Cia., Maximo Gomey (Monte) 466: Casin, Flor de Lobeto.

Rogelio Cuervo y Aguirre, Enrique Barnet 318: La Diosa, Magnolia, Rigoletto.

B. Menendez y Hno., Habana 906: El Rico Habano, Flor de R. Barcia, La Prueba.

C. del Peso y Cial, San Ignacio 314: Flor de Juan Lopez, Flor de Tomas Gutierrez, La Igualdad, Pierrot.

Pita Hnos., Estevez 67 & 69: Caribe, Pita, Pita Hnos.

Agustin Quintero y Cia., D'Clouet 16, Cienfuegos, (Santa Clara Province): El Canon Rayado, La Riqueza, Quintero y Hno.

Juan Cano Sainz, Manrique 615: Caracol, La Flor de Cano, La Rica Hoja, Trocadero.

Oliver y Hno., Segunda del Sur y Marti, Placetas, (Santa Clara Province): La Cachimba, Oliver.

Jose Sixto Valdes, Velez Caviedes 34, Pinar del Rio: Figueras

Simon Vela Pelaez, Juan del Haya--, Pinar del Rio: Gispert.

Rodriguez, Montero y Cia, Encarnacion 163, Santos Suarez: El Trio, La Primadora.

Daniel Blanco y Cia., San Miguel 463: Konuko, Mundial.

Francisco Farach, Marti 24, Caibarien (Santa Clara Province): Flor de Farach.

Pardo, Hno. y Cia., Serafines 164: El Credito.

Julio Gonzlaez, Salud 113: Minerva.

Estrado y Cia., Habana 66, Cienfuegos (Santa Clara Province): Estrada.

Compania Industrial Tabacalera, Cuba 801: Daiquiri, Eloisa, La Bayader, Pirata, William.

C. Rivero Alvarez, Calle 8 #92, Santiago de las Vegas (Havana Province): Fedia, Mi Ideal, Santos Suarez.

Andres Rodriguez Velazquez, Ajiconal, Barrio Paso Viejo, Pinar del Rio: La Dulzura.

Manuel Hernandez Garcia, Velez Caviedes 55, Pinar del Rio: El Campesino.

Roberts & Co., Neptuno 167: Almendares, La Exportadora, Perla del Oceano.

Gabino Campos Beltran, 10 de Octubre 1255, Jesus del Monte: Gabino Campos.

Desiderio M. Camacho, Reparto Camacho--, Santa Clara: La Flor de Lis.

SELECTED BIBLIOGRAPHY

Barclay, Juliet. *Havana Portrait of a City*. London: Cassell, 1993.

Coult, May. *Dictionary of the Cuban Tobacco Industry*. Washington, D.C.: United States Department of Agriculture, Office of Foreign Agricultural Relations, 1952.

Exquemeling, Alexander Olivier. *Bucaniers of America: Or, a true Account of the Most remarkable Assaults Committed of late years upon the Coasts of the West Indies*. London: William Crooke, 1684.

Fairholt, F. W. *Tobacco: Its History and Associations*. London: Chapman and Hall, 1859.

Gill, William. *Havana Cigars*. Havana, 1910.

Gonzalez Baraquano, José, and Jesus Otero Montero. *Santa Clara mapa historico cultural*. Havana: Instituto Cubano de Geodesia y Cartografia, 1989.

Guerra Guerrero, Antonio, and Roberto Fernandez Rodriquez. *Cuba: mapa turistico*. Havana: Instituto Cubano de Geodesia y Cartografia, 1989.

Hazard, Samuel. *Cuba with Pen and Pencil*. Hartford, CT., 1871.

Infante, G. Cabrera. *Holy Smoke*. London: Faber and Faber, 1985.

Knight, Franklin W. *Slave Society in Cuba During the Nineteenth Century*. Madison: University of Wisconsin Press, 1970.

Leal Spengler, Eusebio. *La Habana, ciudad antigua*. Havana: Editorial Letras Cubanas, 1988.

Lobaina Galban, Merle, and Raul Valdes Munoz. *La Habana rutas de omnibus*. Havana: Instituto Cubana de Geodesia y Cartografia, 1988.

Mari Machada, Juan A., and Luis N. Hondal Gonzalez. *El cultivo del tabaco en Cuba*. Havana: Editorial Pueblo y Educacion, 1984.

Martín Zequeira, Maria Elena, and Eduardo Luis Rodriguez Fernandez. *La Habana colonial (1519-1898)*. Seville: Guia Architectura, 1993.

Masse, E. M. *Isle de Cuba et La Havane*. Paris: Lebegue, 1825.

Muñiz Rivero, José. *Tabaco: su historia en Cuba, 2 tomos*. Havana, 1964.

NG La Banda. *Los Sitios Entero*. Qbadisc 9002, New York 1995.

Nuñez Jimenez, Antonio. *The Journey of the Havana Cigar*. Neptune City, N.J.: T. F. H. Publications, (n.d.).

Perdomo, José E., *Léxico Tabacalero Cubano*. Havana: Comision Nacional de Propaganda y Defensa del Tabaco Habano, 1940.

Ortiz Fernandez, Fernando. *Cuban Counterpoint: Tobacco and Sugar*. Translated by Harriet de Onis. New York: Knopf, 1947.

Stubbs, Jean. *Tobacco on the Periphery: A Case Study in Cuban Labour History, 1860-1958*. New York: Cambridge University Press, 1985.

Venegas Fornias, Carlos. *La urbanizacion de las murallas*. Havana: Editorial Letras Cubanas, 1990.

Werner, Carl Avery. *Tobaccoland*. New York: The Tobacco Leaf Publishing Co., 1922.